AR
HUMAN
SOUL
ENERGIES
RECYCLED
BY THE
FUNGI?

We have much to learn from Nature's Recyclers

By

Herb M Cohen

World Journey

Bergenfield, New Jersey

ARE HUMAN SOUL ENERGIES RECYCLED BY THE FUNGI?

———

We have much to learn from Nature's Recyclers.

Herb M. Cohen

Faith, Love, and Hope

Faith of consciousness is freedom
Faith of feeling is weakness
Faith of body is stupidity.

Love of consciousness evokes the same in response
Love of feeling evokes the opposite
Love of body depends only on type and polarity.

Hope of consciousness is strength
Hope of feeling is slavery
Hope of body is disease.

From
All and Everything or
Beelzebub's Tales to His Grandson
1964 Edition Page 361
Author: G. I. Gurdjieff

Are Human Soul Energies Recycled by the Fungi?

Copyright © 2023 by Herb M Cohen

World Journey

Title: Are Human Soul Energies Recycled by the Fungi?

ISBN: Paperback 978-0-9822323-8-5

eBook   978-0-9822323-6-1

Library of Congress Control Number: 2023920787

First Edition, 2023

1.1

Author Online @ Youtube.com/herbcohentaichi

Other books by the author:

"Journey to Feel like a Man" 978-0-9822323-3-0

"The Soul of Nature"   978-0-9822323-0-9

Acknowledgements

Echie Mendoza, my partner

For continued support and encouragement,
and the suggestion for the title.

Jeallian-Colline Mendoza, for Cover Art Work

Jeallian sent these 4 references to document how she created the cover image.
Each of the source photos are available, for free, to modify and combine into new and original works of art.

https://unsplash.com/

https://unsplash.com/photos/JXUfF7HYfMo - man
Photo by Guido Blokker on Unsplash

https://unsplash.com/photos/7qhL24a3kLs - fungi
Photo by Guido Blokker on Unsplash

https://unsplash.com/photos/HWXSmUoP66E -background
Photo by Adrian Pelletier on Unsplash

Jeallian can be reached at:
'jcolline.m@gmail.com'

Steve Fajen My ace in the hole. Whose ear was always open, and his mind too.

Andy Loose and Abigale Great willingness to help. Especially with presenting the attention exercises.

Contents

Foreword

What inspired me to write this book was a documentary I saw that depicted something called a 'biome' extracting nutrients from one tree and transporting them through its roots down into the earth, which is the biome, and then up into the roots of another tree. So, the nutrients, which were radioactively tagged, travelled into the biome under the ground, and then up into the roots of another tree, where the tagged nutrients were found, offering proof, trees communicate with each other. In this way the biome was helping both trees to become part of a healthier forest. Fungi in the soil served a symbiotic function for the forest as a whole. Thus, nature functions as a trinity of forces to maintain and sustain life. The two trees are the active and passive forces, while the fungi act as the reconciling force, or Holy Spirit for the forest. This is a fundamental process that repeats itself throughout all scales in our universe. In our human gut we have many millions of particles made up of bacteria, viruses, and fungi, called the microbiome.

Our microbiome helps us stay healthy by keeping us in harmony with our surrounding atmosphere. The microbiome particles are not human genetic, cellular material. These particles come from the atmosphere surrounding us at the time of birth. And they remain with us for the whole of our lives, always working to keep us healthy. These particles integrate with our human immune system. The microbiome particles residing throughout our bodies weigh a little more than half our overall weight. So, a more accurate picture of our bodies could be described as an organism made up of human cells floating in a sea of biome particles. It would also be accurate to say all life forms on earth are made up of their own genetic cells surrounded by biome material.

Although I am not a biologist, I have had a decent education, but, I have never been so aware of just how integrated we all are with our surrounding atmosphere. Somehow my mind began to think about the idea of a soul. This biome was sounding like a soul to me. If there really is such a thing as a soul, how would it work? Remember, the soul is not a physical organ in our bodies, the soul is a human concept in some people's mind, used to give meaning to certain human actions and feelings, that otherwise, would be extremely difficult to explain. Am I just imagining it, or could there really be some parallel between these two concepts, the biome and the soul? That's what this book is about.

Before seeing videos by Suzanne Simard, 'The Hub-Tree Documentary' and the 'Fantastic Fungi' by Paul Stamets, I had no idea that the recycling of life energies is carried out by one of our oldest classifications of life, called the biome, which consists of fungi, bacteria and viruses. Fungi are one of the first life forms to inhabit land on earth. And fungi were there to help the algae coming out of the sea, to establish themselves on land. The fungi were established on land perhaps a 100 million years before plants began to arrive. So, the fungi have had a very long time to evolve their evolutionary skills. And the most important skill is symbiosis, which gives fungi an extraordinary ability to successfully stimulate the growth and development of surrounding life forms.

I thought things just rotted by themselves. Kind of like the treatment of garbage, you throw it out, a truck comes to pick it up, and then it gets thrown onto a huge pile called land fill, which is buried with more dirt covering it up.

But that isn't what happens when we die, at least not to most humans where I live. Whether you are buried or cremated, eventually our remains end up in different parts of the atmosphere, including the earth itself, and depends on the chemicals contained in our corpse. There can also be differences in corpses because of what has been eaten, or factors of health or disease. But, could there be differences because of intense thoughts, or beliefs, or special practices done during our lives? More about this later on.

The most important factor, is to realize that the Biome is capable of acting in a symbiotic way toward the corpse, whether it is a dead tree, a dead animal, or a dead person. The Biome serves nature symbiotically, both during the life of an organism, and also after it dies, by sending materials where they belong, in the greater scheme of things. This sounds like the soul's function to me.

Another marvelous example of the power of this symbiotic function involves a Hub tree. A Hub tree is the oldest tree in a forest, like a mother tree for that forest. All the trees in this forest have identical DNA, so it functions like one whole individual organism, and the mother tree can be hundreds of years old. As the hub or mother tree approaches death, which itself can take hundreds of years, it begins to give up its carbon to other surrounding trees. Researchers found about 40% of the Hub tree's carbon was passed on to younger trees. If the death process of the Hub tree were to be cut short, let's say due to logging, a proportionate amount of carbon would be wasted. The Mother tree seems to show concern for the future of her forest. Isn't that what our soul is for, our future?

Why would this be an interesting comparison to make? Because, in my opinion, first, if there really is a true basis for comparing the biome to the idea of a soul, I would rejoice in the discovery that the soul, as the term is commonly used, has a genuine counterpart in the world of nature, which, according to my definition of a soul, means I am somehow accountable for how I live my life; and second, it tells me there is significant value in the fact that nature provides us an opportunity to make a difference in the world, by making certain choices, rather than other choices. And third, if nature has already included choice in evolution, and in particular my own personal choices, I am not alone in the universe, because the laws of nature are available to help, if I can comprehend what those laws are. Then, if we really have souls, I would say it is good evidence that life cannot be meaningless. And that would be profoundly gratifying.

Introduction: What is a Biome?

Many people are not familiar with the term Biome, I know I wasn't, so I will begin with a layman's version of what it is, and how it relates to why I am writing this book. If I was a biologist, I am sure this introduction would be very different.

I am also sure most people are familiar with the term, ecosystem, which means a biological area or environment in which each species of plant or animal performs some function that helps the entire environment survive and even thrive. This function is called a symbiotic function. There can be one or many such functions supporting survival of the overall ecosystem. A Biome is also an area or environment that could contain one or more ecosystems. So, it could be considered a large or very large ecosystem.

Being a large entity, a Biome includes biological features such as, seasonal temperature ranges, amount of water available, different terrains, such as forests, grasslands, mountains, deserts, soil types, sun light, wind and more. By studying biomes scientists hope to discover key elements in the dynamics of why and how they survive, and how we humans could make useful changes in these systems if needed, especially when human modifications to these environments have already created negative influences.

So far, I have only been looking at what a biome is from its most external, whole aspect. The term biome also has a very internal, microscopic aspect as well. We humans have in our gut what we call a microbiome. Our gut contains approximately 70% of the biome material in our bodies. The rest of the biome material in our bodies interact with our immune system to help keep us healthy. In total, biome material accounts for more than 50% of our body weight. So actually, we humans and every other species of animal life on earth carry about half biome material, and the rest is RNA and DNA cellular material, specific to the genetics of each species. Biome material consist of fungi, bacteria, viruses, particles and chemicals such as phosphorus, nitrogen, carbon and more.

Scientists are very interested in studying this inner aspect of the human biome because they realize it is the source of many potential discoveries in the world of antibacterial and immunotherapeutic agents. Some scientists hope a second Penicillin-like medication will be discovered there. The biome can be viewed as a great ally in the worldwide battle against disease.

Already I feel I have touched upon the first of several reasons I am writing this book. I am simply amazed to find out we humans are composed of around half foreign substances called fungi, which live and exist in what is called a biome. So, we are not made up only of cells with human RNA and DNA. Within our bodies this inner biome, called a microbiome, residing mostly in our stomachs, aid our health through the digestive system, and by interacting with our immune system as well. Even though we are a unique species of life, we obviously require significant help from the fungi, which is an entirely different class of life that also inhabits our planet.

I never before experienced the fact that I am not only part of animal life, but that I also belong to the world of fungi. Prior to this I thought life consisted only of plant and animal life. I knew there were germs before, but I never felt they were part of me. As it turns out there is still a lot more to discover about the significance of this Fungi world within and surrounding us.

In today's world the scientific community is seeing a great resurgence of interest in studying the biome because our government is currently lifting the ban on studying psychedelic producing fungi or mushrooms, which are all part of the biome. If you remember, the 1970's brought in the advent of LSD and psychedelic trips, which scared the wits out of many people in powerful political positions in our country. But now with the legalization of Marihuana, doors to research are opening again.

This is an excellent example of the importance of public awareness having a powerful effect on the direction of scientific research and social thinking in general. In my personal case, recent documentaries on the significance of the Biome and Microbiome, have had an enormous influence on how I think about many things I had already been studying for years.

One of the most important is how I pictured the evolution of life. I thought the main elements were, having sufficient Oxygen in the atmosphere, temperature, water, plants, animals and ultimately humans. I never heard of or was aware of, any intermediating element such as the Biome, and the whole world of fungi. I always thought life consisted of two main kinds of life, plants and animal life. Now I hear and read about a third Kingdom, the Fungi; and learn that the fungi world communicates with the plant kingdom through mycelium fibers, which are finer than our human network of brain neurons, to create symbiotic pathways among trees in a forest.

Fungi networks fill the earth almost everywhere, and penetrate tree and plant root systems. Fungi then transmit nutrients from one tree or plant to another, wherever it is needed for a symbiotic effect. Considering the biome world of fungi as a Third Kingdom of life, adds a new dimension to our vision of the great scope of influence fungi might have on nature. Here I am referring to far out possibilities, such as effects on the earth's overall consciousness, and influence on higher dimensional worlds, such as the whole earth itself, and even other planets of our solar system and beyond. Atmospheres surround almost every entity in the universe, from moons, planets and suns to molecules and atoms. So, our biomes, which are made of earth's atmosphere, should feel right at home exchanging materials, perhaps even esoteric rays, like a form of cosmic rays, how about, biome rays.

Perhaps we will discover the reason psychedelic effects are even possible. Could the extreme old, evolutionary age of the fungi, have something to do with its psychedelic potentials? Remember the remark attributed to Albert Einstein, 'humans use less than 10% of their brain power'. What would it mean to increase that amount? Could psychedelic effects have something to do with using more of our brain power? The psychedelic effects of mushrooms can sometimes lead searchers into the study of meditation, which is another approach to exploring the possibilities of becoming more sensitive to the potential power within ourselves as human beings. And since meditation can be practiced without psychedelic chemicals, the apprehension and danger concerning the use of powerful chemicals can be avoided. Meditation can have an effect on one's inner state of being, and when it does, it provides a very fresh view of whatever is perceived by one's attention during those moments.

Modern science, in all fields of study, concentrates its efforts on obtaining objective, verifiable results. So, the methods of gathering data must be external with respect to the researchers. All data has to be entered into a computer. By the very nature of this approach, data is separated from the actual moment of experience by the living researchers. The practice of meditation provides a totally internal experience of perception. Granted, the meditation approach is also totally subjective, but by itself, this does not disqualify the impressions so gathered from being noted. When many individuals report the same subjective impressions repeatedly, the validity of that data or information, becomes more acceptable as a valid source. When, on a walk through the forest, the walkers all report seeing roses, one would also expect to see roses while taking that walk.

The point is science needs to appropriately broaden its parameters for gathering data. With regard to subjective experiences, we may never be able to externalize them entirely. And perhaps there is no genuine need to. Some experiences happen only once in a lifetime. And all efforts to repeat them fail. Consensus of common experience can be accurate and valid. Meditators often share experiences with other meditators because people who do not practice meditation cannot relate to the sharing of this kind of material. It's not snobbery, or thinking meditators know better, it's just that there is much more common ground between meditators. Don't forget, in many instances cooperation is a more powerful force of evolutionary change than competition. What is necessary to acknowledge, is that inner experiences are part of the natural reality of life. In olden times people were much more aware of this fact.

Another class of experience we need to become more sensitive to has to do with recognizing some experiences seem to have a higher kind, or feeling of energy. And the causes of these more intense experiences also have to be explored more deeply, and not just dismissed or ignored because they are difficult to classify. There will be more about this later in the book.

Fungi systems also act as recycle agents when trees, plants and animals die. This process creates new soil for future ecological growth. From human corpses, this recycling function may also release higher energy elements, if and when they are encountered. In this sense the recycling function may perform a vital role in transmitting esoteric materials to unknown places in our universe. In the Gurdjieff system, these elements are sometimes referred to as 'Higher Being Bodies'. Currently, some Christian sects speak of the possibilities of Sainthood, which implies a certain degree of spiritual attainment above the ordinary. Eastern religions and Buddhist teachings also contain concepts of higher spiritual development. If someday these ideas can be made more scientifically acceptable, this area of possibilities could shed light on genuine processes of higher energy phenomenon going on in our universe. If evidence for higher energy waves or particles are found, parallels might be discovered between the soul and the biome.

The soul, in concept, is supposed to transmit the qualifying deeds of the diseased, in some form, to some place, where they might be able to continue their meritorious service to the universe. Once 'qualifying deeds' are defined in terms of measurable energies, by our investigator scientists, we could trace biome effects. The biome releases all materials, including those 'qualifying deeds' from the corpse. Some chemicals certainly return to earth to replenish the soil; some may rejoin the atmosphere where they came from, and the 'qualifying deeds' could theoretically go where they must go, to fulfill their destiny.

The exploration of recycling functions may provide insights into why many ancient cultures put special emphasis on significant funeral procedures, forms of esoteric preparations, and also generated concepts of possible afterlife scenarios.

It is also currently thought that fungi made it possible for the first algae coming out of the sea, to establish itself on land. The ability of fungi to help with this process may have been its prime ability, to penetrate solid rock with its own mycelia, and turn rock into soil. Which, is precisely how fungi established their own place on land, many millions of years before the first algae ever appeared.

So essentially, fungi were on land perhaps 100 million years before plants or animals. That is a long time to practice survival in an evolving world. We humans have been around only about 3 million years.

And for the last 5-10,000 years we seem to be concentrating more on what we are capable of, rather than on what nature might need. During the last 500 years or so this trend in human activity has accelerated with greatly increased neglect for nature's needs. This of course, coincides with the development of global industrialization.

The addition of a Third Kingdom, the biome with its fungi, creates a significant trinity; plants, fungi, and animals; whereas before, most knew only the duality of plants and animals. Adding to the picture, the human takeover of life on the surface of our planet, brings us closer to a profound need to comprehend our planetary role. Maybe these are just my feelings, but without fungi in the picture, I can easily relegate plants to the farm, and animals to the pasture, but I cannot harvest the omnipresent fungi. Without fungi there is no trinity, perhaps no life at all.

What seems extremely significant to me is that mushrooms, from the fungi world, are the life forms that produce psychedelic experiences. No matter what you may think about the value or morality of psychedelic experiences, in the scheme of nature, from descriptions of these experiences, you have to admit the effects do represent the involvement of some kind of higher, or unexplained energy. That many older civilizations and cultures all over the world made spiritual use of these experiences, for whatever reasons, cannot be disregarded if we wish to arrive at some comprehension, of what higher energy forces may signify, for the full human experience of life. I have been practicing different forms of meditation for over 50 years, how would my efforts compare with psychedelic experiences?

Search the Internet to find out more about Biomes. Use words like: biome, microbiome, fungi, evolutionary biology, etc. ...

Chapter One
Can Life be Wonderful in Our Eighties and Beyond?

I am talking about being equally exciting, interesting, and as challenging and rewarding as any other stage in life. Of course, each stage has different and very distinguishing characteristics. Biologically and in conjunction with evolution, each stage is essentially preparing us for the next phase. Do you feel the stage of Old Age is as equally regarded as each of the other stages? In America today, I think our old age is neglected and undervalued. We don't seem to have any reason to respect this final stage, we even fear it.

It's the only stage we feel we could do well without. As far as we know, nothing seems to come after it, so what's the point? Does death have a purpose? Is there something our old age should prepare us for? Does death have a follow up experience?

An appropriate understanding of death is one of the things most missing, and ignored in our modern, scientific, industrial society. Life appears, and enters where our everyday senses can perceive it, and after death, we recognize life disappears from these senses. So, from this superficial perspective, the life cycle appears complete, or so it seems. To the senses, life simply comes and goes. Is it any wonder depression abounds? ----------------

I wish I could say I believed in an afterlife. I would like to believe, but I am really not sure about all that. And I am certainly afraid, that there may not be. So, what do I know? I know our ordinary, everyday, sensory experiences, are not the only possible impressions of life human beings can have. We are a life form that exists on more than just this one level of experience. "Human beings do not live by bread alone". And if we never experience anything of a higher quality, I would say we have missed something big in life. Experiences of higher emotions such as feelings of love, gratitude, devotion, loyalty, friendship and others, are clearly composed of more vibrant energies than the lukewarm impressions we feel every day. And the mind, our real mind, not just our talking head, is certainly capable of far more than we use it for, most of the time. And even our physical sensations are capable of their finer moments. And as Neil Diamond says in his song 'Nothing but a Heartache', "But getting by don't mean your living".

Its why Nature continuously evolves, and why each life needs a Soul, to point the way. When scientists, or anyone, claim all of existence is just an accident, without any direction, they greatly over-state the validity of their evidence.

That Nature, has assigned Fungi the job of recycling all energies symbiotically, to help maintain evolution, is evidence to me that the concept of a Soul belongs to Nature, as much as it does to spirituality and religion. So, as spiritual traditions define the Soul, old age is its most fruitful time for development, rather than physical youth. Older age is when we have the most time available for the inner work of prayer, contemplation and meditation.

Take notice of the ecstatic delight of young infants when they experience events entirely new and fascinating to them. Our everyday world is an entirely new cosmos to them. It is only as our senses become dulled by surrounding negativity and spiritual neglect, do many of us succumb to experiencing life as something ordinary, and dead in spirit. When we catch moments of being alive, as spectacular experiences, it makes us aware of a realm of existence above ourselves.

So why do we fear death? Animals fear it too. If they see it coming, they run or fly for their lives. Fear of death is the most essential instinct driving all of evolution. No living creature wants to die! We all try to avoid it. On the other hand, from my observations, I don't think animals imagine about death or conjure up fear about it the way many humans do. This kind of fear, when there is no present danger, can cause much depression and harmful negativity. For some it has developed into a kind of negative obsession, with no clear way out, having no cure but death.

I wonder if our great capacity for imagination, is likely reason humans can have a strong tendency toward obsessive depression about death. By greatly increasing the size of our cerebral cortex in a relatively short space of time, about 3-4 million years ago, nature enabled human beings to reach our current level of intellectual as well as technological achievement. The power of human imagination is driven by the capacities of our enlarged cerebral cortex. But given the present chaotic state of our social world society, it seems to me we might be experiencing significant, negative side effects from this unique gift.

Animals don't have the great capacity for negative imagination that humans are burdened with. So, for those who suffer from this kind of fear of death, I can see why they would not joyfully accept Old Age as a phase of life. And I even wonder if our overwhelming willingness to engage in constant warfare, throughout world history, isn't also somehow related to our preference to willingly avoid old age. Is it possible we fear the process of getting old more than death itself? Why would this be? I think we might try to enjoy life more. But I don't think that possibility is happening. Maybe that's why our religions of the world, and they have existed in every society; always picture their heaven, as a joyous place. So, it looks like there is one thing we might agree on, i.e. being a little happier in the here and now. May I add, how wonderful it might be to have a happy Old Age.   And wouldn't that include coming to grips with death along the way? And that's also what this book is about.

I reached my biggest goal of becoming a fencing champion when I was 24. But the fire that fueled that aim was soon to go out. Then I had to face the struggle to make a living. I managed to do it, but it never brought the thrill and excitement I got from fencing. So, I also found ways to coach fencing, and that helped keep me sane. Next, I discovered Tai Chi, which had a slow-motion form of practice as well as a martial art fighting part. I met many Chinese who did the slow- motion part well into old age. It was referred to as "moving meditation". And in the Gurdjieff work I also got into sitting meditation. The point is, now at 83, I have plenty of experience in many interesting things I can still do very well.

This is what a path in life means to me. Everyone can make one to suit themselves. But you do have to have good luck and the opportunities. In that sense you have to be smart, remain alert, and not be too lazy.

However, development of the Soul is not something we really have any control of. No matter what life puts in front of us, how we face it, not the outcome of events, determines whether our Soul develops or not. How our Soul develops will always remain one of life's great mysteries. The only thing we might be sure of, is that if fear dominates our state of being, especially at the time surrounding death, we might experience regret. Just as if we felt we were dying too soon.

Keep in mind, from retirement age of around 65, till death around 90, that's 25 years of not having to work every day. That sounds like bliss to me.

Chapter Two
The Trinity Model

Traditionally, spiritual beliefs, guided by religious teachings, which have always been part of every culture, are intended to reconcile, what is a natural fear, with the reality of inevitable death. In earlier times, before modern science, the approach to understanding spiritual questions was often based on a concept of Trinity. But nowadays, we don't hear too much about the idea of Trinity, except perhaps in a religious or spiritual context. The idea we are more familiar with is Duality; good and bad, success and failure, rich or poor, war or peace, happy or sad, dead or alive, etc. etc. ...

Therefore, I wish to illustrate with a few, hopefully, clear examples, what a trinity is, and why ancient and traditional societies may have developed this approach to try to understand some of life's greatest mysteries:

Our Solar Trinity: Three Cosmoses simultaneously
Our Solar System, Active force, Sun
Our Earth,   Passive force, Micro-Biome, Fungi
Life on Earth,   Reconciling force, Human Beings

Evolution   Consciousness evolves:
Active + Passive =   Reconciling
Reconciling + Time = Evolution
Evolution + Time =   Toward Higher consciousness.

Holy Trinity: Judaism, Christianity, Islam
              Father   Active
                Son   Passive
            Holy Spirit Reconciling

Heaven   Affirming
Hell   Denying
Purgatory Reconciling

Daoism:
    Yin   Passive
    Yang   Active
    Whole   Reconciling
    Higher Consciousness
            Nirvana (some eastern teachings)

Force One, Active, Able, Mind, Father:
            Spiritual belief, Religious Teaching,
            Consciousness
Force Two, Passive, Reaction, Fear, Habit, Child,
            Son, Daughter, Obsessive, Reflex,
            Automatic Behavior, Depression
Force Three, Reconcile, Neutral, Harmony,
            Patience, Heal, Holy Spirit, Love,
            Understanding, Compassion, Faith,
            Death, Rebirth, Evolution

One   Active, Teaching, Mind, Awake, Cure.
Two   Passive, Body, Fear, Sleep, Disease.
Three   Reconcile, Life Experience, Death,
            Survival, Healer

Earth Trinity
            Atmosphere   Air   Reconciling
            Earth   Land   Passive
            Sun   Energy Active
        Air   Active
        Forest   Passive
        Rain   Neutralize

Evolution = Consciousness Evolves
 Biome   = Atmosphere
First Life = Single celled creatures
        Multiple celled creatures
            Fungi, Mushrooms
                Ocean plants
                    Land plants, Photosynthesis, % of Oxygen

increases in atmosphere
Sea animals, Fish
Amphibian animals
Land animals
Dinosaurs
Mammals
Humans, Cerebral Cortex
expands in size

Inner Trinity,
Mind of Being (not talking head, or
associative thinking, or day dreaming)
Feeling awareness, breath
Body, presence
Meditation, to be still, striving to experience
the whole, to be, is.
All three experienced simultaneously,
become One, Whole.
One center, day dreaming, pain, hunger, happy, sad.
Two centers, self-remembering, self-aware, mind & body,
Three centered experiences, Gratitude,
Humility, Peace, Compassion, Joy, Love.

Life Trinity,
Birth	Positive
Lifespan	Reconciling
Death	Negative

Plants   Active (absorb CO_2, make O_2)
Fungi   Reconciling (symbiotic with Plants & Animals)
Animals Passive (absorb O_2, make CO_2)

The above is not gospel, so think about it, disagree, and improve it. My point is Nature seems to have an agenda for increasing consciousness. Instead of consciousness you can also call it, higher degree or level of Intelligence. You can also say, if a person reaches the full experience of this state of Inner Trinity, they have reached a higher level of understanding. Or, you can say, at the moment of reaching that state they probably comprehended a lot more about the meaning and purpose of life than I do.

Then, in modern times, science comes along to offer a different approach to this fundamental human question of, how did we get here, and what are we supposed to be doing here, if anything?

Science's concept, simply put is, "everything that exists came about by accident". There is no such thing as anything higher, meaning everything is made of the same particles, the only differences are in the combinations which result in many varying properties, and there are only 3 dimensions plus time as the 4th dimension.

There are no such things in Nature as Love, Soul, Conscience, Purpose, Heaven, Hell, or Creator. Life just happened, like everything else, even our consciousness is an emergent property of life, that continues to evolve without purpose.   Like everything else.   Even the universe itself will disappear in about 4 or 5 billion years.

The above mentioned, special attributes, are made-up human terms, to help us think and believe we have the answers for these mysteries, even when what we really need is the humility, courage, inner strength of character, and intelligence to see the truth; that we are still very far from knowing all there is to know about these mysterious properties.

And, to take it even further, we have to recognize that some older civilizations may have had a deeper, and more profound understanding of life and existence, than we do today, in spite of all our technological advances.

However, when both traditional, and modern scientific approaches to solutions, fail to serve their purpose, we may develop intense fear, and obsessive behaviors to fill in for the anxieties produced by this lack of comprehending ultimate Truth.

Without some understanding of ultimate truths, and without really knowing, as we pretend, we do, it's no wonder humans seem to flounder, and remain underdeveloped.

Some people give up, just shrink back to the perceptions of their own five senses, and refuse to believe anything exists beyond that. Most, probably try to live with the uncertainties, and continue with their lives as best they can. And there are even a smallish number, who at times devote themselves to varying degrees of serious study into the question; is there anything real, hidden within a mysterious, spiritual realm.

In this book we will create scenarios that offer an understanding of death's role in Evolution, without making any assumptions about God. Our concept is based on biology, and on the concept that under 'certain conditions', the natural process of recycling, performed by the Biome, will produce evolutionary results. (See Pg 23)

And especially with humans, there is a great parallel, between how far in advance of all other species we are during life, and therefore, also, in the death process, we may have a broader range of possibilities for evolving than other species.

What I am putting fourth is the idea that the Micro-Biome within us, might be seen as the soul. Or at least, it might be a transmitter of soul material, through the atmosphere to wherever Nature needs it to go.

Chapter Three
The Spiritual Principle in Recycling

Evolution is already a proven fact of Nature. Note, here I am not referring specifically to Darwin's Theory of Evolution, but to the fossil record that so clearly lays out a path toward increasing intelligence over time, culminating in humans. Remember, even though we may be accustomed to seeing life and evolution around us every day, both are extraordinary events. Life and evolution are both on-going miracles. Maybe that's why, so far, we only see these processes on our Earth, in Our Solar Trinity.

So far, we have presented a picture of our modern world as being in deep trouble spiritually, scientifically and socially. For me, the proposal of the role of the Biome as a transmitter of soul material explains how nature connects all of life's creations, especially humans, with the esoteric side of the evolutionary process. I am using the term 'esoteric' in the sense that it represents a deeper, more hidden aspect of an evolutionary process developing consciousness, throughout the entire universe.

I quote here from one of my favorite books,
'The Cloud of Unknowing' a fourteenth century English book written by an anonymous monk.
(**see Bibliography**)
"God is the essence of your soul, as your soul is the essence of your body." ... "No name, no emotion, no thought is more like the everlasting nature of God than the experience you have, see and feel in the blind and loving observation of the word *is*." (Cloud Pg 183-184)

-- ---------

We need to define three things as clearly as we can. First is consciousness, second is evolution, and third is the universe. What we experience as being alive, knowing it, in any dynamic moment of time, can be our working definition of consciousness. Its full definition can include a much broader range of contemplation. So, at the very least we can say, consciousness is the most fundamental, basic property of living things. The amoeba has it, just as the human being. And, at death, the property of consciousness seems to vanish, as far as a human observer can tell.

However, for a moment, let's think of the difference between the amoeba and the human being, with respect to consciousness. The difference is enormous, at least three dimensions, or maybe four or five. And in Nature, now that life, and also human life exists in the universe, all of these levels of consciousness exist together, at the same time, in each living human being. You cannot say that about any other species of life on earth. Now, human beings include all levels of life that came before. This is the result of the transcendent properties of evolution, how evolution affected the development of consciousness on the earth. And the story is on-going, within each individual human being, as well as in each other species.

Evolution is a process affecting the existence of all matter in the universe. Evolution takes place in time, and a lot of time can be required to witness its effects. All living matter exists in an environment finely tuned to its precise needs or requirements. As changes take place in the environment, caused by continual movement everywhere, evolution determines whether or not any given life form will continue to exist. Evolution is a process that experiments with the balance of the desire to live, with the necessary force to survive. As long as the result is survival, its action is considered symbiotic. On the earth, the world of Fungi seems to act as an agent of evolution. But circumstances can always arise, where a species dies out.

The universe contains everything, all forms of matter and all forms of energy. Even anti-matter is part of the universe. Humans have determined the universe began at one precise moment in time, some 14.7 billion years ago, and still continues to expand today. The universe has continued to expand from the moment it appeared. Humans know this happened, but we do not know, for absolute certain, why it began. But we do know, pretty much, how. And the fact seems to be that the same rules or laws, governing the expansion, are still in operation today. These basic rules or laws of nature worked with virtually no consciousness for eons, i.e. the first 7-11 billion years, thus producing a random, lifeless universe. But today we have to add, the newcomers, life and consciousness, which began around 3-7 billion years ago. This latest development is the opportunity for the human race.

What is important to realize, is that even though all the same forces exist now, as have existed for the last 14.7 billion years, what is new, is that living matter, or life forms, have begun to exist on our planet earth. Of course, we are not sure if this is also true somewhere else in our universe or not. But as we know, life began to appear on earth around 3 billion years ago. And this, is a really big deal!

Life, especially human life, and in particular our industrial age, is having an enormous effect on earth's environment. Our power machines and computer systems are compressing the time scale needed by our natural environment to be able to deal with this accelerating rate of change. It has only been within the last 20 to 30 years that humanity has begun to accept, that we have to make major adjustments to our industrial life style. To replace our current fossil fuel model with a longer term and less destructive, sustainable model, has just begun to be recognized as a necessary, essential goal, rather than a merely, more expensive means to a less profitable end. So, the next 20 to 30 years will reveal humanity's response level. And of course, extinction is always a possibility at any time.

On the positive side, this is not the first time our human life style has been threatened with a dire need for serious change. Our current situation seems to be very much in keeping with how nature lets us know something is going wrong in our environment.

An earlier example, is the profound and relatively sudden growth spurt of the human cerebral cortex, which took place around 3 million years ago. Scientists are not certain why it took place, but it was responsible for a rapid development of mental skills, which had a relatively sudden, advancing effect, on development of the fossil remains of human societies. Why it was needed may still remain a mystery, but clearly the effects it had are still very much with us today, meaning our technological advances.

The paradox is, there has not been a corresponding leap forward in our feeling or emotional part. Not yet anyway. Today humans have excellent mental powers, but a level of emotional maturity, more appropriate to wild predatory animals. There are always exceptions to the rule, so on an individual basis there may be many human exceptions, but on the level of society as a whole, violence and petty hatreds rule. In terms of survival, our animal rivals today, are no match for us, and cannot restrict humans in our aims, or in any of our activities.

However, there is another looming, possible avenue of threat to our absolute rule over life on earth, and that is the small, microscopic worlds of insects, bacteria, viruses, and fungi.

Currently, our human 'Will' is unopposed on the earth. We have heard distantly about the Black Plague, almost forgotten the Spanish Influenzas, and are only reminded of it because of today's Covid19 pandemic. So, we are still beyond the reach of any restraining influences, except from other humans, although, we cannot be sure for how long it will remain as it seems today.

So, perhaps in our current period, with regard to our evolution, we are at a somewhat awkward stage. Our thinking part has overwhelmed our emotional or feeling part, and has led to today's world-wide obsession with technology. This same imbalance of mind over feeling, has also led to other seriously negative social results in many parts of the world. And there is no way our human civilization is about to voluntarily change course.

Unlike our friends the fungi, whose main approach to survival, with the help of about 300 million years of practice, seems to be symbiotic, our human approach is still competitive. Which might explain our quick response to fight, or go to war. We haven't yet reached that stage of evolution, where we can employ symbiosis, as the way to move forward. But maybe it's not that simple either.

Each passing day more people are becoming alarmed about all the warning signs of global warming, and our need to reduce the amounts of harmful chemicals we are putting into our environment and ourselves. So, maybe our human civilization will begin to modify its course, and actually prove able to avert impending disaster. The challenge to survive this immanent threat, and other, even more deadly ones to come, may actually provide the impetus, to make that emotional or feeling leap forward, that has been missing.

This is evolution in action, how it really happens. After centuries of lopsided momentum in a seriously violent, disturbed direction, nature calls us to task; either clean up your act or perish. We are speaking here of an undertaking that, could require most of our civilized attention for the next 500 years or so.

The Hidden Aspect of Recycling

Recycling appears on earth with the death of the first cells, or particles of living tissue, that were the original matter awakened to the startling new experience of life. The beginnings of life marked the origin of an unbroken chain of living, related, atoms and molecules. With the passing away of each new life, a new arrangement of particles was possible, based on the previous arrangement. And the new arrangements were always subject to change. Once life appeared, new life was exposed to variations in its surroundings.

What human event could you consider hidden? You the reader, must be open to contemplate, what is this question asking? So please, stop for a moment, until you have arrived at some ideas of your own, regarding what kind of events might qualify as hidden. ... ...

Appreciate, at that very moment, on our planet Earth, the first experience of life enters existence, appears in time, the first instant, the first moment, an impression, a memory. Time as we recognize it begins. A new dimension is added to the planet Earth, in this Solar system, in this Galaxy, in the entire Universe. Where did this event come from? So much was here before, maybe 8-9 billion years of early earth development.

But that was without consciousness, without experience. No memory. So, what can we call this unique, brand-new moment? Miracle? Luck? Accident? God? Does it really matter what we call it? I don't know.

Hidden, is a something I do not have an answer for. I can only say, I do not know. Can I say it is a mystery? Why not? Does it help me grasp that there are events, properties, circumstances, situations, I have no explanation for? Can it be as real to have no explanation, as it is to be full of explanations?

This is what it means to me, to be 'hidden'. Or what the word 'esoteric' means to me in the context of 'deeper meaning', rare, or more profound. What about in our own lives? Do I ever have moments where I experience, not knowing? Where my mind, my whole sense of presence goes blank for a moment. Where I cannot explain what I am experiencing? Where I may experience, I don't know who I am, or where I am going, or, that I expect something that does not happen, even when I was so sure.

I speak here about the absolute necessity to have your own personal experience, of something, not ordinary. We all experience the ordinary world at every moment, however, that's not quite true for some. In order to be open to the possibility of other worlds, another world, perhaps a hidden dimension, an unexplained energy, a unique incident with time, or with memory, you have to have your own experience of it.

Only if you truly believe, every single moment of your existence has been ordinary, in the sense that there is nothing else to understand or experience, then I would ask, why are you reading this book? Otherwise, let's continue.

When fungi do their job on living things, they apply symbiotic means to improve the health, and well-being of their biome. When they work on dead things, to recycle materials, they still apply symbiotic principles. We know that with trees, fungi create renewed soil to be used again for the benefit of the forest. What is the result when fungi recycle people? For one thing, if the corpse is underground, renewed soil would certainly be one product. But could there be other products as well? Remember, here we are comparing the biome with the concept of a human soul.

The traditional function of a soul, is to measure the deeds of an individual, according to specific traditional beliefs, and store them in the soul. At the place of judgment, also only a concept of each tradition, they receive a fair and just evaluation, so the remnants of the former person will in some form, be able to go to a suitable location. In terms of opportunities for consciousness, this new place may be better or worse than their prior lives on earth. And, in terms of their continued participation in the universe, they may have more responsibilities or fewer. And in almost all traditions, this is when each soul finds itself with company, similar to itself, in terms of the measure of its soul.

Wouldn't we just love to know exactly which chemicals to store in our souls? And how to store them there. If only it were that easy.

When fungi begin to breakdown the materials in a corpse, what guides them? What might they be looking for? In chemical mixing, the results will always be the same if the chemicals are always the same. When fungi apply symbiosis during the recycling process, are the results always the same? We know when recycling takes place in forests, fertile soil, is one result for the next generation of forest life. We know there are many kinds of fungi, and perhaps each one performs different functions, and corpses can have different materials also, depending on their lifetime experiences. So, not all functions will be activated by each corpse. But where would re-cycled human chemicals end up? That, I don't know.

The greatest differences between each human corpse might be in the area of psychic manifestations, such as levels of consciousness, intensity of memories, or other qualitative merits, such as good deeds, or acts of kindness. If the corpse qualifies, an equivalent chemical, or emotional energy is deposited in the soul. Theoretically, I would expect to find significant differences in the area of emotion, and feelings, as manifested in the lives of different individuals. Earlier in the book I mention that if "certain conditions" were met during the recycling process, evolutionary changes could be triggered by the fungi. This is what I was referring to. But clearly, in terms of any specific chemical, I do not have answers as to what these "certain conditions" might be. (Ref Pg 17)

Here we need to consider training practices from spiritual traditions, which claim it possible for humans to train their attention, to reach detectable levels above ordinary. If this could be shown, it would support the concept of inner psychic development that Buddhist monks, and priests, and others, have been working towards for centuries. In olden times, traditions would judge individuals, by certain traits of external behavior, and inner bearing, to certify that certain achievements had been reached. But even though this may not be externally provable today, there are those who believe sufficiently in this possibility, to be working in this direction.

The Gurdjieff system puts forth several main ideas, that have been very helpful and even sustaining for me. In ordinary life we are relatively asleep. Like using only 10% of our brain power. As I write this I wonder, why doesn't this saying, or any like it, inspire us in an active way? To actually do something about it. I think it's because we just take it in with our heads. Any one center, physical, emotional, mental, it doesn't matter, it's still just ordinary, just talk. And we need something stronger, a shock. So, we need to 'remember ourselves' in a much more whole way, which can bring a very different experience from any ordinary moment. This is special, only if the experience lights you up, seeing the difference, between ordinary, and a new reality, even for a moment. That inner experience can be memorable. It can be the beginning of a life-long path to explore new territory.

Another principle, is that we have three main centers of experiencing; the mind, the body, and feeling. Mind, includes thinking, and talking, but mind, in its awesome sense, includes much more as well, for example, contemplating the beginning of time.

In humans today, the mind, with respect to activating its full potential, is the most ignored, and least harmonized part. Any part of the body can be sensed, and the entire body can be sensed as a whole presence. Feelings can be humility, gratitude, joy, peace, happiness, sadness, grief, courage, and more. And emotional reactions like, anger, fear, annoyance, impatience, insulted, happy, depressed, self-righteous, intimidated, guilty, ashamed, bullying, and more, are all part of our emotional life. It is important to distinguish between one's own feelings, and one's emotional reactions. As we are, without the proper training, we may not be aware of the true origin of these responses from within us. And they may not all carry the same quality and value of feeling energy from the viewpoint of universal consciousness.

When plants absorb the Sun's energy in the atmosphere and generate O_2 from photosynthesis, do they utilize everything in the air? No, they select only the CO_2; not all the air molecules are used. Likewise, perhaps not all our emotional energy has the same value for the universe, and is able to provide symbiotic energy to the universe. And who is it that makes these distinctions? The Fungi world!

The Gurdjieff system also makes a very useful distinction between plant, animal, and human life forms. Notice, that Gurdjieff makes no mention anywhere of fungi, as far as I am aware. In his time Fungi were included as part of plant life in biology. Plants, animals and humans represent three different levels of being existence. This refers to three different levels of energy or consciousness.

However, mankind in our current, average state, is not considered to be fully developed or evolved. Our typical thinking and talking state, does not utilize all the energy it is possible, or even proper for us to have. In Gurdjieff's view, we are considered, incomplete beings. We must 'work' on ourselves, to raise our level of consciousness, to become more complete.

Each species as a whole unit, plays a significant role in the maintenance, or balance of energies in our universe. Plants represent the energy role corresponding to the body. Animals, the role of the body with the feelings. And humans, the role of all three together, body, feeling and mind.

Plants have harmonized with nature primarily through their body function. Animals have a brain, but their brain is not nearly as well developed as a human's brain. So, animals cannot harmonize with their minds as humans potentially can, but are very similar to humans in relation to the body and to feelings. Humans are potentially able to harmonize fully with all three centers, but if we don't, we cannot fulfill our loftiest role in life. Because we are not harmonized sufficiently, chaos rules our world-wide society.

In the tradition of Christianity, the depiction of Jesus Christ provides the perfect example of the way all human beings should be capable of living and behaving. Only with this as a perspective, can we recognize how great our shortcomings are.

The fact that our civilization has managed to survive and multiply for over 2,000 years, in spite of our shortcomings, also has to be recognized. So, as serious as it may be, human kind has not failed yet. And it is up to as many as possible, who wish to awaken to a higher truth, to make it happen.

Plants fulfill the functions nature has given them. Animals also fulfill their natural functions. Humans do not fulfill our natural functions entirely. This is not a popular assessment of human behavior. Most people would not accept this as a valid description of ourselves. So, only those who, at least to some extent, are willing to accept our own dire shortcomings, can I expect to continue bearing with me, on this journey.

When I see how mechanical I am in daily life, I begin to agree more, with this description of experiencing only one center at a time. And as time goes on, I feel happier to be seeing the difference between reality, and mere conditioning. Little by little I want more. A special effort has to be made in order to reach a more united state, which Gurdjieff calls a state of 'self-remembering'. And take note, this special effort is a life time's work, which some say, can even take longer than that.

The active principle is that, at our level of experience, these three centers or energies appear to us sequentially. This is our usual perception of time; ordinary time is sequential. 'Remembering oneself' is at least two centers together, when centers are aware of each other, head or mind, with body, for a moment. It may not sound like much, but when you experience this brief, dimensional change, you will understand better. Each time you try to have it again, our ordinary ego interferes, so each time it has to be as if, for the first time. It's not easy. We all need a strong ego to deal with life, but it doesn't help here. I can write, let go of your ego, but to really experience that, you have to figure it out yourself. This experience is considered a giant step, each time it occurs. It never seems to happen often enough. A three centered experience, stops time in the moment. It is very rare.

It is my thesis that the fungi might be sensitive to these different kinds of energy experiences stored in the body during life, and then activated according to their specific energy properties by the fungi, as part of a mysterious recycling process affecting our souls. I do lots of exercises to increase the awareness of my attention, in the hope it will affect the content of my soul, and bring my subjective energies closer to their full potential, whatever that might be.

Historic Influences to Consider

Suppose, in employing symbiotic means to resolve their problems, one or more earlier civilizations on earth, were more successful than we are today. They would have had the advantage of being closer to nature, as it was on our planet before industrialization. So, they might have enjoyed a more spiritual, emotional life, because of their vulnerability to great nature. Perhaps they wouldn't have had our machines and power tools, to give them that sense of control we love so much. The fact that no such civilization clearly stands out to verify this hypothesis does not nullify the amazing, ancient ruins found all over our planet, that do suggest some older civilizations might have been much more advanced than we think. Especially in an emotional sense.

We bring up this possibility because we do have much archeological evidence to tell us about these civilizations. Our own European civilization did pick up, and even absorb much information from these civilizations, namely, Greek and Roman, Egyptian, Judaic, Christian and Islamic, and others, but less so. And we are taught very little about the Chinese, Japanese, Korean, Indian, Persian, Tibetan, and North, Central, and South American Indian cultures. Each of these cultures had very elaborate and very individualistic creation myths. Some believed in an original creator, and some did not. But, from their perspective in history, all did try to explain how everything got here.

Not one of them, that we know of, claimed it all happened by accident, or offered no explanation at all. The view that it all came about by random accident, only began to arise with the advancement of modern discoveries, mostly in the European civilization, of the last 500 or so years.

Certain major events had great influence. The printing press gave written communication a leap forward. More people learned to read and write. Languages could be translated. Copernicus, said the Sun was the center of our solar system, not the Earth. That jolted our physical view of things. Then it turned out, our earth was not flat. Galileo said things that almost got him killed by the Church. The established Christian church was becoming the enemy of science. But as the Church spread its beliefs, it retaliated by becoming wealthy, and supporting the modern slave trade, and other very corrupt practices.

But behind the scenes, other powerful changes in the way many people began to think were emerging. New machines and tools were being developed. Guns and cannons needed gunpowder; the machines needed fuel. A great need for energy was altering western civilization, at blinding speed. All machines have one thing in common, they must work. If they fail to be operational, they must be fixed or replaced. If you don't get it working, someone else will. Everyone was in competition with everyone else. The power equipment was evolving in leaps and bounds. Competition was fierce and violent. Duality took over. Reconciliation was for the losers. Either you get the business or someone else does. The operating rule became, either or, do or die, him (yes, masculine only) or me. Symbiosis, got lost in the shuffle, except maybe in houses of worship. But even there, symbiosis was offered only to members of their own church.

The ideals that drove America's civilization, the pursuit of happiness, except for slaves, equal rights, except for Blacks, right to vote, except for women and Blacks, free lands out west, except for Native Americans and Blacks, all contain serious, spiritual contradictions, and severe penalties of conscience. The pursuit of happiness, became translated into the pursuit of money and power. We are still, today, in a stage of denial.

Until we begin to face the truth, and reality of these glaring contradictions, American culture will not be able to move forward to overcome the shortfalls of our national character.

The paradox I speak of, where the powers of thinking overwhelm the consideration of feeling, have been inherited by political America. The modern idea, that the creation was an accidental result of natural forces, is the current belief of probably half of Americans and also half the world's population. The other half, still hold onto older concepts of a deity being responsible for creation. Also, many people throughout history, have always been uncertain about what to believe, and have gone about their lives without much deep personal concern for this issue. However, from a political and institutional perspective, this question has always had a very powerful influence on world affairs.

So, this division generates a natural bias in everyone's viewpoint about how we got here, and we can never be sure who belongs to which group. This puts a subtle, underlying influence, on everything humanity attempts to do. This phenomenon has shifted our understanding of how things happen in the world, from a fundamental trinity principle, to the short cut, of duality relationship.

All machines, computers, and technology, rely on duality, whereas the biological world functions on the basis of trinity. And this affects everyone's way of thinking on a private, subconscious level. So, how can we communicate better with each other? We must learn how to take this situation into account, in order for humanity to survive into the next century.

The difference between duality and trinity is subtle, which means difficult to recognize. So, recognizing which principle we are following, has to be acknowledged before any corrective actions can be taken. We need to make a conscious attempt, to develop objective ways to heal this currently destructive, unconscious division among people. And to begin to do that, we must each be more willing to try, so that we can reach a workable starting point. Like after World War II, when enough influential people were able to get the United Nations established.

We need the fungi's help. Fungi began to inhabit the earth before there was sufficient oxygen to support the plant and animal kingdoms that followed. It is estimated fungi underground networks currently cover about 90% of land areas on earth. It is also estimated forests have been eliminated by about 85-90% across the world. Wildlife have been reduced by about 90% globally. Fish and other sea life are reduced by about 50% so far. Plastic garbage pollutes the seas by some 85%.

The danger of global warming, excess CO_2 and methane, is the threat we need to vanquish, before it destroys our current civilization. From the duality point of view, it is a matter of life or death, success or failure. But from a trinity viewpoint, we must employ symbiotic methods to resolve the problems. Fungi, with their 300-million-year history behind them, are the experts with symbiosis. How can the fungi in the biomes help us?

Every living organism on earth is an energy center. All forms of reproduction require lavish amounts of precious energy. So, Nature has to make every effort to collect as much energy as possible when plants and creatures die. The conservation of energy is a universal principle of physics and biology. Symbiosis exemplifies the natural wisdom of evolution. Symbiosis reconciles death with life, and sustains the progress of evolution.

Only humans have the intelligence to adapt symbiosis to human needs. What should we call this new branch of science?

PsychoBiomism?   MushroomsAnonymous?
HomoEcoLogy? TerraHomoIsm? GaiaHomoGraphy?

UnitedHumanityIsm?   NoWarfareIsm?
SeaLandAirOlogy? PsychoBiology?
SpiritoMaterialism? UnifiedUniversalism?

Or perhaps by studying with the Master Fungi, or a Hub tree, we could learn a great deal.

Chapter Four,
When the need to Change
Directions in Life Arises

How do we get from where we are today, to closer contact with a path, accessible to our common sense, greatest hopes, and also to our highest aspirations. My own search began at the very moment I won the 1964 US National Foil Fencing Championship.

At the moment I won, I stretched out my arms with my foil in the left hand and my mask in the right, and gazed up at the great brick wall in Convention Hall, Atlantic City. Looking up, I asked myself inwardly, what do I feel? An answer came back ...Nothing!!! Absolutely nothing!

This sense of nothingness took a few long moments to sink in. I was expecting to feel like a champion. But I felt nothing. I had always dreamt of becoming a champion and I knew now, I was one. I was deliriously happy I had finally reached my dream. But this happiness was me, Herb of my dream.

What was that first impression of 'nothing'? Did it mean if I don't dream it, there is nothing, nothing in reality, if I don't make it up myself? This moment, this question, changed my life forever. It marked a turning point in my life.

From this point on, the focal point of my life gradually began to change. It didn't happen all at once, but each new thing that attracted my attention was leading in new directions. I was no longer trying to become a champion in fencing. I had reached that and found it wanting. I still loved fencing, but now I was also interested in exploring this unsatisfied feeling of finding 'nothing', when I expected becoming a champion would confirm my inner sense of being a meaningful, significant person. I had proof that winning the championship I aimed at, didn't do it.

Could I find something that would? Little did I know then, that this new path would consume the rest of my life, and expose me to some very interesting and challenging places, internally and externally. The experiences I have encountered and the things I have struggled to comprehend, lead to this book. My qualification for writing is my sincerity to share some difficult subjects, and also to share many of my subjective but relevant experiences. If you are reading this book, it means I succeeded in writing it at age 83, and also received great brain, and feeling exercise for the effort.

All I claim is that I am having a satisfying, meaningful old age, so far. And that all the experiences I mention in this book are true, and all the exercises I demonstrate are my own versions of what I learned at the Gurdjieff Foundation of New York, during over 50 years of study, and from Fencing Master Michel Alaux, at the Fencers Club of NY, and from Da Liu, my Tai Chi Master in NYC, whose exercises I still do almost daily.

And I hope the reader will receive my message, that we live in a world connected by a common consciousness, as well as, an individually cultivated consciousness, potentially created by you and me.

Later on in the book we will pick up the thread of seeing how I evolved, from this huge disappointment, at the winning of my first national championship, to new experiences, I could not have anticipated.

Chapter Five,
Searching for the Potential of Undiscovered Energies

When we are young and intensely involved with all our desires and ambitions, we don't have time, or make time, to reflect on the question of our own death. [Note: As writing, I am experiencing the stabbing background awareness, that many humans are not lucky enough to enjoy such favorable circumstances as I had growing up.] Then we reach our teens and can finally drive our own cars! And go out on dates! For most of us these are not times to reflect. But you would be surprised, even in the midst of all the virulent activity of early adult life, deep down inside, things are registering. We live in the age of 'just do it', 'go for it', in America, 'follow your dream', so negative things or feelings have to get pushed down, but they are there, waiting for a better opportunity to come out.

By the time we reach middle age and begin to slow down a little, we are ready to start enjoying our successes. So, we may not be ready yet, to give up the pursuit of all that fun we have been working so hard for. But, as we begin to perceive ourselves already, passing into what begins to feel like older age, we begin to have flashes of uncomfortable feelings, something is coming, something I don't want to think about. There is unfinished business arising, something not in its right place yet. Humans have a great capacity for worry, which reflects all kinds of fears, and disorganized thoughts. Some like to call it "the middle age crisis".

Some humans, not all, have an almost instinctive need to wonder about matters beyond their own senses. Others, are content to be concerned mostly with what goes on closely around them. And this perimeter can vary greatly with regard to quality and quantity of interests. Some take up hobbies like playing musical instruments, painting, carpentry, golf, tennis, weaving, quilt making, reading, even meditation and yoga, or Tai Chi. Others like to travel, or try mountain climbing or flying. These widely ranging interests can place humans in strange new territories, whereas animals are more homogeneous relative to each other. We are still animals of course, but with the rapid rise of science we have evolved a bit, at least technologically, and have capabilities that extend further, beyond what the naked eye can see. One aspect of the 'middle age crisis' is that a lot of fundamental questions begin to arise from the depths of our being, and if we are lucky, we finally begin to see we don't have all the answers. And the answers we do have, are not satisfying.

In our present time, the world is filled with great contradictions and significant frustrations, right alongside incredible new technologies, difficult even to imagine. Like many people, we can ignore all these troublesome emotions, and just keep moving straight ahead. We may be fairly successful in dealing with ordinary life matters, but it can begin to dawn on us, that our future wellbeing, may depend on more than just having enough money in the bank. Beginning to see those things, we always took for granted, start to slip away from us, can come with great shock and surprise. Who me, slowing down? We can begin to get a little lost, perhaps even somewhat, out of our depth.

We don't know exactly how to think about these new matters, we don't know what we feel, and we notice we have lost a step, are getting stiff, and a little short of breath. It's not necessary to become a body builder, but watch it! For the first time one's health and mental state become issues we have to begin to be careful about.

An interesting thing here is, not so much to look at these unexpectedness's as arguments to win, or problems to solve, but to embrace them as new impressions, arriving because we are now further along the inevitable, evolutionary path of life and existence. From this perspective I am interested in evaluating these newly arising anxieties, and how they affect new anticipations of death and life.

Why is depression so wide spread in this scientific era? I thought we left the Dark Ages behind, with its overwhelming, fear driven, and blind faith. I always experience my moments of truth as enlightening. God and Evolution can only be comprehended with enlightenment. Fear is darkness and the Devil. "A life unexamined is a life wasted." Said, Carl Jung.

This is one of the main reasons I am writing. From early childhood I have never been satisfied with scenarios claiming death to be an absolute end of our existence. Our psychic experiences are material energies, although much more elusive to capture and measure than other less subtle human experiences.

If we can accept that Cosmic Rays from the Sun are continuously penetrating our entire planet, travel right through it, and us, undisturbed, and still not know what function it serves; how can we deny, that ordinary thoughts, and especially moments of insight, or higher consciousness, may also be made of a materiality capable, in some abstract way, of surviving death, in order to continue to participate in life someplace in the universe currently unknown to us? Where are those Cosmic Rays now?

If, what I have just written has any possibility of truth or reality in it, I would then ask; would these 'higher more sensitive energies' that could leap from life, to death, to life, have any connection with my current existence on earth?

I admit, I prefer to put my hope and my faith, in this possibility, rather than in some other scenario, that flatly denies any possibility of such a connection. What I trust here is the principle that, different levels of energy have different possibilities of action, at different levels in the universe.

A GPS has to use high frequency and high-power electromagnetic waves to communicate between our cell phones and satellites in space orbit. But for earth bound radio and TV, the electromagnetic waves don't need to be of such high frequency or high power.

Whereas waves of consciousness or emanations, have yet to be discovered, so they are still a possibility. Gravity waves, and the phenomenon of 'Quantum Entanglement' have only recently been discovered.

In this book we are developing scenarios based on new understanding of the role of the Biome. The Biome recycles all life on earth. Without the Biome there could be no evolution. Without the Biome would we even have life on earth? Up till very recently the Biome has barely been studied, and its role in nature has been practically unacknowledged, and certainly unexamined.

Unlike animals, humans have much greater ability to see certain future dangers coming, and modify circumstances to protect themselves from it. Even though people often don't fully appreciate life, still, there is something precious about it we don't want to lose. It is also true, at some point we may hope to be able to say, now, I am prepared to die.

The fact we humans even ponder these questions of life and death should make a strong case for our being a creature apart, and above, all others on our planet. I even think it's fair to say that what distinguishes human kind most from our animal companions, is the very fact that we do worry about what lies beyond physical death, and are sincerely concerned about not knowing how to approach the question. But I don't expect most people to be interested in these matters, at least not until personally forced into it by death's actual presence.

Chapter Six,
Back to Exploring Life Stages
and the Biome

What about during the embryonic stage? Do we have the same or similar fears of death even before birth? At the embryonic stage, even though the heart is pumping and most reflex's function, escaping from a threat isn't yet possible. So perhaps the fear of death doesn't begin to develop until after birth. It seems likely, fear of death develops in life, from life's many varied experiences. If this is true, a sharp distinction can be made between a live embryo, and a human being, in the full meaning of the term. The human embryo is alive, but has not yet experienced the complete environment. It has not yet met the Biome. It does not know fear or sex, or have the experience of struggling to survive. It is not yet a complete human being.

In some societies high status is given to members who display fearlessness towards death. Other societies, encourage specific skills development, have sophisticated criteria for evaluating individual lives, and prepare for death, with very precise practices. Most religions present ideas that try to help us reconcile our lives with the certainty of eventual death. I believe religion serves an instinctive human need to be in harmony with nature. But religions, like many other human institutions become corrupt, and end up creating more harm than good. But stories like these we already know too well.

In this book we will bring evolution, biology, science, explainable and unexplainable personal experience, insight and common sense together, to help us recognize the need to be more aware of the full significance, and potentialities of the death process. Which just might stimulate a deeper appreciation of the life we have, and not just intellectually.

To assume our own death is not affected by any of our life's actions is an unexamined position. Everything that alters our life, mentally, physically, emotionally, physiologically, neurologically and chemically, may also affect what is deposited in us as we live. The second most important premise in this book is that all memories, impressions and experiences are stored somewhere in our physical bodies. Our assumption is that these energies may include, in addition to many ordinary memories, other energies, with properties still unknown.

This also includes unexplainable experiences we all may have had, which seem to come from nowhere, which we did not make up, did not encounter before, may never experience again, and which often seem to defy ordinary logic, but for some reason, are still remembered so vividly.

Our brain is the most obvious storage place, but not the only one. And we continue to discover more and more about what is stored in the brain. So, the quantity and quality of energies we store during our lives, may very certainly affect what happens to us after we die. But whether we can or will be aware of it, from the perspective of our current lives as human beings, is a separate question, and one that is still unanswered.

Chapter Seven,
What the Biome Does

The most important premise in this book, is that nature herself, recycles all the experiences needed by Mother Nature, to continue her own path of evolution, and perhaps our own as well. And for this purpose, at death, the Biome, perhaps with the help of other parts, begins recycling all the biomatter and human RNA and DNA cells in our corpse to that end.

That the Biome, which is technically not a human body part, has the job of accomplishing the recycling process is an enlightening discovery for me. It is deeply satisfying for me to think, Nature herself, has every intention of making use of my energies, for the benefit of our surrounding world. And that death is merely the beginning of a new phase in the evolving cycle of individual consciousness.

In other words, the corpse does not merely decompose into a vacuum, the corpse's particles actually return to the atmospheric surroundings it lived in during its lifetime. The recycled particles of biome matter and RNA and DNA cells are freed from the corpse to find their way to wherever they belong in our atmosphere, according to the same laws of attraction and repulsion that created life and death on earth. Like drops of water falling into the boundless sea, or in this case perhaps, more like cosmic rays penetrating the earth and our entire solar system.

Our point here is, why should the biome stop at creating new soil? A dead tree is one thing, a dead human may be something quite different in certain vital ways. It is almost obvious that human life serves the earth in a quite different way than trees. The biome serves all the earth's creatures and all the earth's needs. The biome lives in the atmosphere and in every creature that breathes. And our atmosphere is connected to the moon and all the other planets in our solar system.

Chapter Eight,
More about the Biome as Soul

Biome matter begins to inhabit the newly born only as the embryo approaches the birth canal, nearer to the external atmosphere. Here the embryo begins to be integrated into the local surroundings so it can survive, develop, and experience.

If any deaths have occurred nearby, particles from decomposing corpses could possibly come in contact with the arriving newcomer. After all these millions of years of evolutionary development why hasn't nature found a more precise way to begin integrating a new born child into the local environment? It almost seems Mother Nature is deliberately introducing a randomizing factor into the essential integrating process.

Does the fact that Nature does this, help explain the role and function of the Soul? After death all corpses return to the environment, leaving their experiential particles floating around, carrying with them all their past material experiences from their lives just ending. Surely nature could have found a more controlled method to integrate a newborn embryo.

It seems that nature is giving the human Soul a powerful, optional, capability to influence the energy level of a newly born embryo. Crucial choices made on the level of human life can have an effect on future generations of humans. One of the perks of being human, is that Nature has given us the possibility of evolving to a certain degree, within our own individual lifetimes. Perhaps no other creature on our planet can claim that capability. And perhaps only with the assistance of the fungi, is that possibility maintained.

It is also quite possible, the special energies deposited in the Soul of some exceptional human being, becomes of use to the universe in a way completely unrelated to any surrounding embryos, and may be totally unknown to us.

The emerging picture of the Human Soul as a spiritual organ having the capability of developing skills, perhaps like symbiotic sensitivities, or the quality of goodness, or of wisdom, or compassion, begin to sound more like traditional descriptions from our human past. In those olden times it might have seemed more real to attribute these possibilities to some version of God, or many different Gods. In today's world with our much more detailed knowledge of biology, and genetics, it may seem more appropriate to attribute these possibilities to Nature herself. And in our day and age, thinking of these matters as part of Nature, provides a more physical feeling, for the nature of the Soul itself. Now that we can envision the world of Fungi, exercising its symbiotic influence on the surrounding world, the Soul begins to take on a more physical sense of existence. There is less spiritual mystery about saying the fungi act as a soul, or the transmitter of spiritual energy, than that the Soul is a Spiritual entity. Now we can begin thinking of the Soul as having, at least some physical attributes, along with perhaps some, still mysterious properties.

If there is any truth to the possibility that our human Souls could be of good use to newly born embryos, wouldn't it make sense to actualize that process right here, where special experiences of a higher energy level, or symbiotic quality, would be available to become part of the newborn's essential heredity, in the form of beneficial energy from some exceptional human being, who has just passed on.

Does it mean some corpse's biome matter might get into a new, about to be born embryo? Could there be some kind of force of attraction involved? Could we say, through death, the biome matter is enriched, or even made pregnant, and ready to contribute to the birth of a new being? Could there, therefore, be any personal awareness contained in the contents of this biome matter?

Could the three centers, when experienced simultaneously i.e., mind, body, and feeling, have a special significance for being stored in the biome? Here I refer to complete 'inner trinity' experiences. Some who practice meditation, might have inner experiences that standout unforgettably, from the ordinary. And the same kind of exceptional perceptions may occur randomly. Might these exceptional experiences also have special value for the biome, just as they are especially remembered by us, even while we are alive.

I always wondered, if we have a Soul, how it would get from our corpse to wherever it has to go. The biome is a likely answer. Evolution is a dynamically integrated process, manifesting through continuous generations. Like with every life form, human recycling is mandated by Nature and Evolution, and carried out mainly through the dissolving and reconstituting action of the biome with its Fungi.

There is no doubt life, actually Nature itself, is evolving. So, it makes sense that even without artificial intervention, the Laws of Nature make Evolution possible. In the case of human and animal behavior, and also perhaps during fungi activity, when a certain energy, or a quality, or perhaps a skill, appears in a corpse, its appearance can become the natural catalyst required for an individual's evolution.

This might also imply that in addition to RNA and DNA human heredity, the Soul can contribute to an individual's heredity, from outside its own genetic family boundaries.

The concept of skill is not limited to the physical realm, but can also be of a mental or emotional nuance as well. Great physical strength, heightened problem solving, sensitivity to form and color, are examples. Evolution does not occur for each individual at every death. Only when some exceptional, as yet undefined material arises from the corpse, and is transported through the biome to the appropriate place, can it perform the task of becoming some new feature, or trait in a new being. The variations in each individual within a generation helps ensure the survival of that whole generation. Evolution within a species begins with one individual. If the change is successful, it spreads to others, and only then, can gradually become adopted as a species standard.

If anything, the aim or purpose of life's evolution is increased consciousness. So, what actually increases is the amount or level of awareness or consciousness, which represents an increase in the presence of universal energy.

When this takes place on our planet Earth, through the actions of human beings, it is like a tree bearing fruit. We don't need another tree, just more fruit to balance things out. This would represent a meaningful step forward in the process of creation. Ultimately, Evolution empowers Creation, and may reveal new, and unexpected emerging branches of life.

Chapter Nine,
Our View of Life Grows as
we Grow Physically and
Psychologically

We are taught to spend energies in striving to reach our goals without the slightest awareness that there might be more than one possible way to attain most external life aims. When we are young, we often concentrate on only one or a few ways to accomplish things. Our experience may be narrow, but if we succeed, we stick to what works, or seems to work. The point here is, with all its many relationships and interrelationships, life is an amazingly dynamic place, and the more deeply we grasp the whole, the more in harmony we can be with it. And harmony of every kind and degree is a very successful attribute for life.

Our modern society is in serious environmental trouble, explicitly because of our refusal to accept the absolute rule of 'Don't Mess with Mother Nature'. As a society we leap before we look, so we always encounter unintended consequences. What is even worse, our children follow our bad example, which is why we emphasize, at least try to grasp the whole of a thing, before plunging in. The warning is wise, but mostly unheeded, in our egotistic, individualistic, aggressive, capitalistic society.

From my own childhood I have two examples to explain what I am getting at; it reveals a large part of my own personality features of age 11-12: 'We were playing softball; the other team's batter hit an easy infield popup. My second baseman dropped the ball. I was so mad I went over and punched him in the arm.'

Another example: 'At recess in the school yard we were playing punch ball. We had runners on 1st and 2nd and I told Joel, to hit another single, which he did. Then

I punched a homerun, and we won the game. Later that day Joel complained to the teacher; why couldn't he have hit the homerun? Mrs. Raskin asked me to step out into the hallway. She was trying to explain something to me, but I just couldn't grasp what it was. Finally, she said to me, 'Herbert, you have to learn to play well with others.' All I could answer was; 'But we won the game. I had the best chance to hit the homerun.'

Perhaps it's true we have all wasted much of life's energies in trivial pursuits, and now wish we could do something about it. Well, we can do a lot about it, if we have good health, and know how to use it, even, or especially, in our Old Age. We say more about 'useful work' in the exercise sections.

Evidence of my own athletic evolution, is the fact that I not only won Gold Medals in both NYC high school PSAL, and NYU collegiate NCAA level Fencing tournaments, but also, simultaneously won, the Sportsmanship awards, at both those levels. Sportsmanship awards are selected by popular vote among all competitors. Usually, one fencer wins the fencing competition and a different fencer wins the Sportsmanship award. In this case I won both. I gained people's respect and admiration, as a fencer and as a person. I always valued these Sportsmanship awards above the Fencing medals. These examples reflect someone who acquired a greater understanding of the whole, in the world of fencing, as he developed into an experienced competitor.

Outside the world of fencing, however, people did not seem to notice any significant differences in me. I will try to show, how, within myself, as an individual fencer, I was also able to achieve a greater understanding of the whole. But this change, being on the inside, only I could see the details of what was involved. While from the outside, people could only see I had become a much smoother and quicker athlete. My great coach, Michel Alaux, also got much, well deserved credit for making me a better fencer.

Michel observed which tactics I tried the most when I fenced. He then centered his lessons with me around those tactics, which helped me develop an almost supreme confidence in using them. His training involved the inclusion of every possible response my opponents could make, so that in competition I had no fear of not being able to win with this strategy. Especially after fencing lessons, I was still so tuned up while walking in the street, that suddenly, I would feel like a cat. All alert, aware all around me, noises would startle me, and with back up, I was ready to pounce, like I was on a tightrope. Training really does give you new and better abilities, but their greatest effectiveness is limited to the aim of the training.

The strange part is I am not sure what or how I changed. I did feel more aware of certain things, but it was like flashes of perception, strange new experiences, happening very fast, not like thinking about things. In those moments I felt powerful, electrified. No matter what my opponents did, I was ready with a deadly response of my own. Thus, it began to happen at the most intense moments of competition, I would find myself flying, almost reflexively, executing actions that never had time to cross my mind, to score amazing touches. The moment after each of these more elevated awareness experiences, I would find myself saying to myself, how did I do that?", "how can I do that again? I wish I could do that again."

These intense experiences brought me amazing, unique moments of joy, that made me feel, 'life is not just ordinary, sometimes it's extraordinary.'   Without question, I appreciate these momentary experiences in my life far more than all my ordinary moments and memories. It's the extraordinary moments of memory I treasure. Yes, I do wish to know where my treasures of memory will go when we die. Could they be exactly the same as my ordinary memories? I hope not.

As I approached my peak in fencing, from 1960-1964, I am pretty sure, if it could be measured, I would have registered at least a few points above that average of 10%, that is considered par for the course in human affairs and activities. And to this day many of my fencing friends are still amazed at how detailed my memory of bouts and events are from all those years ago.

Chapter Ten
The Biome Connects us to Worlds Above and Within the Earth

After death, while bodily reflexes and even brain waves still show electrical activity, do we still fear death? It seems too late to fear it now. Disintegration has already begun. As we rot, bodily material evaporates into the air and the ground. Most bodily materials begin to change form, and begin the processes of joining with other kinds of matter.

To nature and evolution, birth and death are more like day and night. Human and animal life forms, measure existence in the time frame of days and nights. But nature measures time, in moon cycles and earth cycles around the Sun. And perhaps even more, planetary cycles and Solar system cycles, and still possibly more, as yet unrecognized.

Once we are dead, we enter a world of the biome, the microscopic world, the worlds of bacteria, and fungi, and viruses. How is time measured there? Do we still retain our consciousness and memories? Upon death, we become part of the recycling team.

Our organs and cellular material become food for the biome, and the earth surrounding us. Our biome breaks down bodily material, and frees it from the body so it can take its place in the surrounding world according to its atomic weight, chemical properties, and perhaps other, as yet undiscovered properties. Recall the smell of death.

Chapter Eleven,
Can we Be Self-aware after
Death?

Now, how about facing the real question; while all this recycling is going on, are we, as individuals, once alive, going to be aware of anything, any longer? My short answer is; 'I don't know.' But what this book is about, is the fact that the biome appears to be a plausible vehicle for transmitting everything experienced in this life, including moments of extraordinary awareness, wherever Nature needs it to go, for the sake of Evolution. It gives me great joy to even fantasize about this, as a real possibility, which allows me to say 'maybe life and death do make sense after all.'

Death does not stand alone, it is not the only process involved, it is not egotistic, as in having the final word. I do not feel abandoned. Death leads to recycling, which leads to possible Evolution. I am much less afraid. I am much more concerned about what I deposit in my biome. I am much more satisfied, to contemplate these mysteries of life and death from this natural perspective, rather than from any made-up, human explanations, including my own.

But, these hidden transformations in the biome, take place between death and life, so we don't really comprehend how to investigate all the possibilities there might be here. Since ancient times, religions have given us many possible scenarios for what might happen after death. But at least for many of us, the progress of modern science seems to have killed most of the impact of these stories. Modern science teaches us to look forward to find knowledge and truth. Looking backwards for any real information is discouraged. And for those who try to maintain some traditional beliefs, well maybe it keeps them happy in this crazy world.

However, to accept uncertainty, without a clear understanding of the origins of our existence on earth, is recognizably upsetting. I think the feeling 'we should know', is so powerful, that many people today just simply jump one way or the other, and make an uneducated decision, to avoid the difficulty of accepting that, neither science, nor religion, can truly prove their point of view, not yet anyway.

The truth and result of this is seen in the rampant depression, belligerence, hostility, intolerance, apathy and lack of harmony in our modern world.

In this book we cannot offer proof either, however, we aim to offer possible scenarios that contain common sense, based on plausible ideas, not obviously unfounded concepts, that demand blind or superficial faith. The faith you need here, is faith in your own wish to understand.

Chapter Twelve,
Understanding the Help of
Trinity

Anyway, trying to explain the existence of life with only a two-dimensional cycle of birth and destruction, fails, because it leaves out the third dimension of nature, and the fourth dimension of evolution. If two dimensions were all there were, life and death might be very brief indeed, similar to those 'virtual particles' that appear and disappear almost immediately in absolute vacuum experiments. Any cycle we propose must include Evolution.

Including evolution with life and death creates a trinity; just as the examples, Father, Son and Holy Spirit, and Yin, Yang working together as two forces, to create the whole. Just 'life and death' or Yin and Yang alone, represent incomplete processes.

Another example is today's computers, which operate with code, based on ones and zeroes. They can be very powerful, but to reach a higher dimension of performance the code has to be based on ones, zeroes, and neutral, thus yielding a trinity-based logic, such as is the case for 'Quantum' computers.

Trinity brings about another dimension of possibilities. Saying, 'life, death and evolution', or Yin, Yang and the universe, tells us that the death we see every day is not nature's end. Just as birth is not the beginning, for lifeless matter preceded living matter. Like everything in motion, the material in the universe is evolving. One of the most elegant expressions I ever heard is; 'The purpose of the universe, is the evolution of consciousnesses.' And that is very uplifting, and even makes a lot of sense. Comprehending truth, is uplifting in a spiritual sense, and in that sense, defines the term spiritual itself, i.e. as uplifting.

Another beauty is: The Creator created the universe in order to share consciousness with 'His/Her/The' creation. Human Beings are the main recipients of this gift, for now. Within the scale of Creation, individual Human Beings can evolve, and become like, God, in consciousness. This is the basic idea behind many spiritual traditions. We need to become closer to God, in terms of consciousness.

Father, Son, Holy Spirit.

Mother, Daughter, Holy Spirit.

Awaken, Practice, Wisdom.

We were created in His/Her/The image of God.

Chapter Thirteen
The Ideas of Consciousness and Self-consciousness

Recycling or the role of the biome in all living species, demonstrates the law of conservation of Energy, which is an integral part of the laws of Physics as well as biological Nature. That we fail to recycle vital materials properly is one of the greatest failures of our modern age. We are ignorant, self-righteous polluters. We have religions, we speak of God, yet we refuse to admit how recklessly we are destroying the balance between nature and ourselves. And we are *'strangely blind'* to all evidence, relentlessly warning us that we are not in as much control of things, as we insist on continuing to imagine we are.

Here, we will discuss concepts of consciousness and self-consciousness. But before going further, I must say something about the term 'strangely blind' I use above: This "strange blindness", is a perfect example of a lethal flaw in our personal relationship with nature.

At the same time as we see, hear and discover, more and more about the serious effects of our worldwide polluting, which represents a growing 'consciousness' of the horrendous state of global, human affairs, rapidly approaching, we stubbornly continue to justify our destructive practices. Yet, in our self-consciousness, these facts can seem very far away from ourselves as individuals, and because of that, our whole society is at great risk of neglecting to take adequate precautions on major environmental issues.

Our culture is dangerously divided by this internal conflict. We sustain two major consciousnesses in simultaneous conflict with each other. This is far too strenuous to deal with calmly, so most of us opt to basically, block out one side of the picture altogether. This can blind us in serious ways.

Thus, we can say; 'I realize this dangerous situation, but it's not my fault, or responsibility, so how can I help to fix it'. Thus, a great barrier begins to appear between our consciousness of the world around us, and the self-consciousness, of our inner feelings of righteousness, and convictions of safety. Or, we behave like the Ostrich, who feels safe when it puts its head in the sand.

Consciousness is a huge concept, which includes really everything in the realm of living awareness. While self-consciousness is extremely personal. Nevertheless, in order to maintain a healthy state of mind, body, and especially feeling, the two consciousnesses have to maintain a harmony with each other. These two consciousnesses must discover a way to function as a trinity, and find a healing approach to help resolve this paranoid state of affairs, in which, one part of us sees a serious danger approaching, and our other part wants not to see it.

Technology has inadvertently created other environmental distortions as well. Such as, by using TV, to show people and situations from anywhere on the planet instantaneously, all situations seem to be happening nearby. So, our ordinary, everyday sense of time and distance has become distorted.

Showing people suffering in different ways on worldwide TV, allows us to see and hear situations, but does not give us the same kind of impressions we would have if we were actually there in person, at that location, with those people. The temperature, the wind, the smells, the moods, and other human factors simply cannot be conveyed on TV. Being there in person might be contrasted with going to see a live play on Broadway, or watching a movie. TV is not real life, even though the color, sound and size of the screen are wonderful.

However, because we are becoming more and more accustomed to accepting our impressions of life through the TV, we begin to accept those impressions as if they were real life. So, in actual fact, we become comfortable substituting the TV impressions, for real life. Which means our true reality is becoming comprised of less than all the vibrations making up person-to-person contact. TV, whether watching for pleasure, or information, or for business purposes, by its very technological nature, distorts the contents of traditional human contact and communication. Even Zoom meetings, which I love, or any other TV communication medium, can never be a true equal to person-to-person contact. If you disagree, take the difference literally, compare the TV signal with a human presence. If you still disagree, you would probably do well to renew some non-electric acquaintances.

Some, so called primitive societies, clearly evolved over a long time period, more in harmony with surrounding nature, than our own current society. This may be so, simply because technological development was at a more primitive stage than today. Or perhaps because today we view high technology as the only signs of true knowledge, and ignore, other possible indications of advanced culture found in older civilizations. Many older cultures had great reverence for the wisdom of their older populations, which may have contributed to their cultural stability and deeper appreciation of life. We recognize that warfare has always been a part of human history, but the more rapidly and more totally we are capable of destroying each other, obviously, the greater is the danger.

Other modern trends may also be having their negative impact on the communications experience. The impression of time passing, has been affected by the high speed, compressed, loud presentation of deceitful sales campaigns and news presentations. The fast tempo of information absorption, has affected which parts of our bodies are, or can be receptive in the act of absorbing information. A slower tempo might make use of deeper, more sensitive parts of our feeling centers. Modern technology, intentionally, forces human beings to adapt to the technologies, rather than to make learning experiences richer, more complete, meaningful and enjoyable for the audience.

The presentation of all public media has to be strictly edited to fit into precise time-frames. This is having a negative, still unrealized effect on our population. Its impact will only become more visible with time, and is way beyond the scope of this little book.

Our being out of harmony with surrounding nature, and also not in harmony within ourselves, is centrally relevant to our theme, of not respecting the stage of Old Age, i.e., our 80's and onward.

Our high technology should be able to provide at least most of the world's population, good health and living conditions, so that retirement age could begin around 60, with an average life span of 90, would give us 30 years to pursue whatever pleases us most in life.

As long as we would be in good enough, overall physical shape, why wouldn't this be a greatly looked forward to period of our lives. Of course, the life choices we make would always be dependent on how wise and appropriate we were. Judging by myself, I am 83, I am really getting into meditation, and doing exercises that involve utilizing the attention in an active way. This is why I have included videos of all my favorite forms of exercise in the book.

We all have problems, last year I was diagnosed with a Melanoma, which was excised successfully, and now I am under medical surveillance for the next few years. But gratefully, I am not handicapped in any way, yet. So, I continue exercising the body, took on the challenge of writing this book, which is a big challenge for my mental functioning, and I am loving it. My Old Age is fantastic, so far.

We have to remind ourselves we can always find people worse off than ourselves, and also better off than we are. Very few things go perfectly in our lives. And even when they do, it might not last for too long. Mature people try to make the best of whatever difficulties they are forced to face. And are always alert to recognize good opportunities to pursue their own favorite interests.

I have a few friends who are not doing as well as I am. I keep trying to encourage them, but most of us are deeply rooted in our own life patterns. And there are some things we cannot change.

Chapter Fourteen, Everything is Connected to Everything Else

I think at least part of the problem is that up till very recently recognition of the biome, as an equal shareholder of the vital functions, in the main spheres of biology, was not recognized. What I mean is, if we list the main realms of biology, we would get a list approximately as follows: Earth, Minerals, Water, Fire, Air, Plants, Animals, Humans and Evolution. The materials that make up the biome, might not even be mentioned. Yet it is a very distinct sphere of biological activity.

Environmentally, the biome engages with the embryo as it merges with life on the planet. No life of any kind exists without a biome. The biome is like the anti-matter to matter. As life emerges from the womb, the biome welcomes the new born with a whole menu of essential particles that allow it to survive in this new, utterly foreign world. Biome matter shares space with the human cellular material of the body. But biome material itself does not contain any human DNA. As life goes on these diverse materials, cells of DNA and biome matter, continue to mix and blend with each other within the organism's body.

When death occurs, the cells and matter of life's processes are recycled by the fungi and particles of biome matter within the body. By volume, there is more biome material in the world, also in each of us, than human cellular material. All material, like cells, blood, organs and bones, exist within a sea of biome matter inside each individual creature. The breakdown of life materials into biome matter does not take place in a vacuum. It does not happen by itself.

Rotting is one of the biome's main jobs. The biome is a sphere of matter that exists to maintain cellular life in a healthy condition, while the creature is alive, and after death, to recycle cellular material so it can re-blend with surrounding nature. It is an integrated element in biological evolution. Without the biome, evolution, next year's crops, etc.... would not happen.

Nature seems most interested in evolution, and not so much in the life of any one member of any particular species. Could it be said that Mother Nature utilizes the biome to help prepare material for evolution, while leaving the job of cellular procreation to cellular beings? Could the biome be seeking after human bodily material, capable of becoming biome material? Remember, the biome is not human material, and does not get born with the baby, but enters a new-born from our atmosphere. And assuming Mother Nature has a fundamental need for conscious material, or material with properties of a specific energy, decomposition extracts those materials from the body for possible use somewhere in the biome atmosphere. Also remember, our atmosphere is not here just so that we humans can breathe, but it serves other purposes as well, such as photosynthesis, as one example. We are also discovering almost everything, both living and not living, have atmospheres, and exist in atmospheres.

What we need to grasp, is that death precipitates evolving life; for better and for worse. Changes in the environment are passed on through the biome. Yes, also through Genetics, via RNA and DNA, etc.... but what genetics affects, takes place within a newly conceived life form. Whereas the decomposing actions of the biome occur after death, and before new life appears.

Perhaps the evolutionary changes made by biomes, don't appear only on the surface of our planet, like renewed soil, but rather, appear somewhere else in our atmosphere, currently, completely unknown to us. The biome's role in evolution may be more spiritual than we ever imagined. Dare we say, considering the biome to play the role of a soul, may not be entirely without merit? And also, may be closer to the traditional conception of a soul having something to do with representing higher spiritual attainment.

Sperm cells swim through the Biome Sea, which is not human RNA and DNA cells. It is through the action of the biome that new life gets its opportunity. And this does not happen only in the realm of our three-dimensional senses, but may affect esoteric properties in our atmosphere as well. The biome is like a realm of inner space. Every cell in our bodies exists in the Biome Sea. We once thought outer space was an empty void, but currently we realize it is never actually empty. Virtual particles are always appearing, from who knows where, and then disappearing again into the unknown. This is where the biome, and perhaps life itself is quite mysterious. We don't know everything that happens in the biome interaction with our human RNA and DNA.

We know that our brain records most if not all our life experiences. Experiences of consciousness are also recorded in the brain. But I am not sure in what form this might take place. And how would the biome break down experiences of our consciousness? What kind of matter would that create? Would that matter become involved in creation of the next generation? I think these are some interesting questions.

Recent discoveries in the life of trees, and how forests develop, reveal how underground root systems create clumps of trees that communicate with each other and aid each other to optimize mutual benefits. The tree roots blend with fungi, a biome substance, and generate communicating systems among diverse tree species for the best foresting results. Planting just a single tree, or the same plant species over a large space, does not yield optimal results.

Keep in mind that with all animals, including Humans, the biome contains the results of all chemicals produced during all experiences undergone by that living creature. So, we have to ask ourselves, do all different experiences leave the exact same chemical traces in our biome. Could certain experiences be different than others in terms of what they deposit in their biome? Is everyone's biome identical? Is everyone's life identical? Through death and recycling, the material of everything gets redistributed as far as allowed by chemistry and the laws of Physics. But do we really have any accurate way of determining what that means? This is the field of Evolutionary Biology, a science that studies the effects of the biome and ecology on evolution?

Whatever you might think is the degree of difference between animals and humans, I am sure you will agree humans are far more complex in experiences and behaviors than any other creature on earth. I regard all forms of life as have varying degrees of consciousness, and also self-consciousness. Human consciousness, and especially human self-consciousness rank at the top of the class, and far above any other creature in the rankings. With that, humans can be very good, or equally very bad.

Some humans are highly intelligent, others very average. Some are great artists or musicians, others not so great. Some are very strong others not so much. Some short, some tall. We come in different colors too. And some have a high degree of self-consciousness, while others are just average. And in the expression of each of these categories there can be great differences, which emerge during the lifetime of individuals based on many factors such as, heredity, environment, accident, necessity, and intention, through practice and learning. Human societies have always admired great skill and invented elevated categories called artist, scientist, genius, athlete, musician, master, healer, or chief, etc. But not everybody reaches such heights.

Chapter Fifteen,
Trying to Understand different
Levels and States

And the point is, if the biome is the medium through which our reabsorbed particles are recycled, our further destinies may reflect our present lives as individuals. I have no idea where we will go after this life, but if the biome has anything to do with it, we will go where our particles can continue their existence. How much consciousness any particle will have I don't know, but I think it might be a good idea to strive to have as much consciousness of everything we can, while we are still in this life on earth.

With regard to most of these categories of similarities and differences, there are many combinations which make up the complexity of life, and most of us already understand this. What needs a little more explanation concerns the category of 'self-consciousness.' This is a more complex and less easily explained characteristic. Simply put it means 'awareness of self'. Consciousness is very similar to awareness, which can also be taken simply to mean having a sense of knowing something about the universe, or oneself.

Example: As I walk through a forest, suddenly I notice or become aware, or conscious, of the fact that something has scraped against my arm. I may react by turning to look at where I feel pain, or heard my sleeve tear, or to see if I am bleeding. Or I might call out, 'Oh my gosh, what happened', and with my other arm reach around to try to see what happened to my arm and sleeve. And there can be many other possibilities to describe such situations.

Other words I might use are, 'perception' or 'impression' or 'experience'. Perception or impression, are words we use to describe 'our sensory registering of an event affecting me at this very moment'. It is actually a very complex event, and has many possible variations.

None of the possibilities are right or wrong, but all reflect precisely who you are at that moment. And depending on the exact nature of the kind of event we are considering, it could include one or many moments in time, either continuous or separate, and even simultaneous, meaning many different events within the body, happening all at the same time.

We have to define various perceptions or events so that we can develop a clear method for communicating about our experiences. Communicating personal, unique experiences to other individuals is extremely difficult to do. That's why when it is attempted it is usually with people who share a great deal of the same or very similar experiences. Here we are not trying to clarify experiences for their own value or meaning. Can we find a way to share our perceptions, impressions, or experiences, so that we can communicate through common, recognizable conversational expressions?

For example: Pain is sensed as in the body. Fear or a fright evokes an emotion. It may last only for part of a second. Anger may combine an emotion and a bodily movement of arm or leg. Joy or satisfaction may evoke a moment of emotional happiness, and may be followed quickly by thoughts and imagination concerning the event. Sexual attraction can be clearly experienced as a moment that can become many other things very quickly. But that first moment is distinctly remembered. The main point is we need to make these categorizations as clear and simple as we can. The complexity comes because we are capable of experiencing many impressions very rapidly and often simultaneously. And it is essential to be able to distinguish accurately from where they arise within the organism. Centers of emotion, thought, the body, or sex, or feeling, or mind can be identified and located.

> i.e., chest or heart, or solar-plexus,
> head or brain,
> brain or imagination,

body or breathing, or stomach or leg.

The singular most important result from this kind of analysis, is to try to become able to distinguish between a response that represents the whole person, rather than a reaction that clearly represents only a fractional part of the person. This will never be an easy analysis to make, objectively. But the aim is to develop some kind of perceptive skill, that recognizes the whole, as opposed to only a part of people, including yourself.

To be able to accurately discern this difference between the whole and a part from within yourself, is considered one of the centerpieces of spiritual work in the Gurdjieff teaching, and is called 'observing yourself', or similarly 'remembering yourself'. If you are able to work on this with other interested people, you will want some way to have a consensus on different evaluations, so you can discuss them together.

Using the example of a walk in the forest; at the moment we become aware of something scraping my arm, my body has made me aware of an unexpected and possibly dangerous event. The body is designed to do this. The response of the body makes you aware of pain. That gets the attention. The movement of the arm reflects possible mental training in first aid. The comment 'oh gosh' may reflect a mental or emotional fear reaction or attitude. The attention to the danger of a possible wound, blocks out all other possible needs I may have at the moment. All the attention is on what I must do about the wound. I am not aware of the whole of myself, in this moment, but I do not know this in the moment. The attention is mercurial, in the next moment it is somewhere else. Awareness can move very quickly. But in that moment my wound can seem to be all of me.

What is so interesting here, is that this little scenario could also play out almost as its own opposite. The brushing of the arm against the tree branch could cause a response from the body as a whole. Maybe the person has special training, and in this moment happens to be very attentive and awake. The response is very calm, I become aware of the pain, and everything seems to happen in slow time. The scrape is examined carefully with the other arm. No bleeding or serious harm is seen. We can continue on. But I need to be more careful. I smile to myself.

There is nothing obvious about one's state of presence. A quick response can represent great presence, or just as well a frightened reaction. The difference lies in whether the parts blend together or act separately, which affects our impression of the overall event. Life can happen so fast I can only have a full evaluation after the event. Yet in the very moment of happening, I live the event to the fullest, aware of everything, with no contradictions, an impression of unity, leaving a vivid, clear memory. Afterwards, at a much slower pace, in a familiar, ordinary state, I review the memory. Now, this is just the ordinary, everyday mind, at work remembering a past event.

Chapter Sixteen,
The difference between the Power of Words and the Power of Attention

During a recent TV interview, I heard the renowned Astro Physicist, Neil de Grasse Tyson, kind of cry out, "we are all made of stardust" almost pleading, and imploringly asking, why doesn't that fact help us realize how much we are all really related as human beings? And why doesn't our science have a more beneficial effect on human interactions. I too, wish it would. Why doesn't it? Because hearing, or speaking words, does not automatically elicit life changing perceptions. Any impression powerful enough to change a person's life, in whatever form it might take, would be an overwhelming, unforgettable, experience. Note: like my experience the moment after winning the 1964 National Fencing Championship, (ref. Chap 4 Para 1)

Unlike the saying, "in one ear out the other", impressions of a life changing power, would be recorded very differently, wherever they might be stored in the body, mind, or heart. The point is, since all human perceptions are stored somewhere in our bodies, and passed on to our biome as some form of energy, our biome would recognize each of us as individuals, according to our unique lifetime perceptions. Thus, it is, that our biome might be the agent of leaving our perceptive legacy to the universe. If we had "souls" perhaps it would be through the biome, the souls would get passed on to wherever nature needed them to be.

humans support the earth, growing in consciousness: a note

Chapter Seventeen,
The Esoteric Aspect of Skill Development

I am using the term 'esoteric' in the sense that it represents a deeper, more hidden level of skill development. We all have to develop certain skills just to live and survive. An esoteric level of skill would be a self-perceived level, recognized from within, as far superior to other good, but ordinary skills one may have. The inner impressions received during moments of experiencing a higher state of consciousness, accompanied by an extraordinary skill occurrence, may be very unusual, surprising, and also unforgettable.

One might even experience a complete separation between body and spirit, like I once did. While another person might have similar experiences, but refer to it as 'muscle memory'. Which description, I find degrading. Merely because one does not know what it is, to call it 'muscle memory'. When I say 'a complete separation between my body and my spirit' I realize, I am describing a subjective experience, I cannot explain.

To be the best of the best; among the many great basketball players, most would agree Michael Jordan stood above the rest, he was an esoteric player. Bill Russell had unique, esoteric skills as the greatest defensive player ever. In a New York Times article, when asked how he was able to keep himself motivated when playing for 8 championships, Russell replied; I was no longer playing to win games, but was carried along by the high-level play of the other great players on the court with me. But I could not communicate this motivation to my teammates, they would think I was crazy. Wilt Chamberlain spoke of his experience of playing against Russell with profound respect and gracious humility. Chamberlain averaged 12 or 13 points per game against Russell. In the International world of soccer Pele was esoteric, he stood all by himself, even with three men covering him. Or Babe Ruth, or currently, Tom Brady, LeBron James and Stephan Currie. As for the rest of us, let us strive to be as great as we can become, with emphasis on the becoming.

During my freshman year in college, I began to become seriously interested in becoming a Fencing Champion. My success in high school fencing made it clear to me that Fencing was my sport. I had natural aptitude for it, and also saw that being a little on the short side of height (5' 7.5") alone, would not prevent me. To make the U.S. Olympic Team, and maybe to become U.S. National Champion, became very attractive goals. Becoming an Olympic or World Champion seemed a little out of reach, mainly because we recognized the Europeans to be a level better than us. And this was because at this point in time, we hardly ever travelled to Europe to fence with them.

There are two different aspects involved in my pursuit of this aim. One has to do with my ego, my vanity, my sense of pride and fantasy. More than anything else, I wanted everyone to recognize what a great fencer I was. And of course, to my Ego that meant, who I was, that I could be great in something. I had fears of losing and fear I would never reach my goal. But in this book, that aspect is not the one I wish to concentrate on. The question here is, how to become the best possible at whatever you choose.

This aspect of pursuing an aim is really universal, and is about unlocking the secrets of ones chosen skill or art. The reason skill development is highly regarded all over the world, is that each unique skill represents, in miniature, the greatest path of all, the path of becoming perfect, the best, ultimately, the perfect person.

In fencing, your opponent is going to try to hit you with the sword. So, if you can, you must try to hit your opponent first. Alternatively, you must prevent the opponent from hitting you, if you can. All training is about, if you can; whether that means sink the basket, make a touchdown, hit a homerun, make the batter swing and miss, paint a portrait that everyone recognizes, play Beethoven's 5th symphony on your violin, build a table everyone admires, or in fencing, make a touché, a clear and decisive one, that leaves no doubt as to who would be dead, and who would remain alive.

One day my teammate, Jerry Halpern and I, went up to the third-floor gym, which we would have all to ourselves, to practice. We knew each other since high school and fenced many times. Jerry is tall and has a very natural and loose style. We get en-gardé and start to fence. Jerry makes a leaping fleche attack, straight at me, and hits me on the chest. What! I say to myself, how could he have hit me so easily, and I get en-gardé again. He does it again, I try to parry, but before my foil blade can parry his attack, he hits. Impossible! I say out loud, nobody can hit me like that. But he did!

I was really shocked. If Jerry could hit me like that, many others could do the same. I had to see exactly what was happening. I immediately said to Jerry, let's do that again slowly, I have to figure out how you were able to hit me on your straight attack. There was no trickery involved, no deception, no strategy, just timing, he hit me before I could parry. Why?

We repeated the action several times. I began to examine the situation in minute detail. As Jerry leaped at me, I watched his blade flying through the air, and I watched my foil blade rising from en-gardé position, near my waist, to meet his blade. I saw that I moved my sword from the wrist first, with locked fingers, the blade was trailing behind a little, bam; he hit me before my blade met his blade in the air. So, my hand was there, but the blade was lagging behind. Ok, I am going to initiate my parry from the tip of my blade (35 inches

long) by closing my fingers, to move the blade before I
start moving the hand from the wrist, to make the parry.
Bingo! I watched my blade meet his blade in midair, long
before he was close to my chest. When parrying, always
move the point of the blade with the fingers, before the
hand and wrist.

I immediately began to make this adjustment
with everyone I fenced, in practice and in real bouts. As
you can see, I have never forgotten this amazing learning
experience. And more than once I have been told, my
parry riposté was deadly, like an assassins' strike. I
developed a reputation for being quite ordinary to watch
from the sidelines, but being very hard to hit. And I
cannot help but thinking how many trained fencers I
met, who were not aware of this simple secret, and how
much of a negative effect that had on their results.

This story is an example of how a simple
technique can become the basis for evolving to another
level. The concept of there being different levels in
everything, is vitally important. You need to be able to
recognize, in your own experience, and from your own
perception, what level you are on and how you can reach
the next level up. There is no side-stepping the fact you
cannot beat anyone on a higher level, except, when
beating them also means you are reaching that next
level.

Now, let's look even further into how I discovered
what is involved in trying to reach a higher level in
fencing, and how I gained, unexpectedly, and only much
later, insights into the significance of the trinity concept.

As a rising young star in fencing, I was trying to
beat all those athletes ahead of me, who had already won
many of just these same tournaments I was now trying
to win. Fencing is a very complex sport or art. It's combat
without getting hurt. However, there are rules about
how you are allowed to move forward, and backward, left

and right, ducking and using the non-sword arm and hand. But there are no height, weight or strength restrictions, so you have to face all shapes, sizes and builds, and left and right handers.

The challenge is how to beat fencers who are better than you. Let's first look at what prevents you from beating them now. When you try to attack, they are able to parry you, and score with their riposté. Or you attack and they jump back out of distance, you can't reach them. They attack you and score. At this stage it's very depressing! You feel quite helpless. But this stage informs you of just what it means to be one of the best.

You keep trying, you increase frequency of lessons, and, you have to have a fencing master or instructor, who is good enough to help you get better. If the teacher is good, your attack techniques will become faster and smoother, and strength and footwork will improve. It is important to start getting a few more touches on some of the better fencers, but you have to go beyond that.

The next stage of practice and training requires very attentive experiencing of everything going on within your mind and body. So, in practice, you need to observe mind, and body, but add feeling when trying to implement advanced techniques. When practicing, do not concern yourself about winning, concentrate only on successfully executing the specific strategy you are trying at the moment. Trying to win practice bouts too soon is the most common mistake I have seen fencers make. You must recognize and respect, that there is a transition you have to be able to make, between learning a tactic in the fencing lesson, and in doing it successfully in a practice bout. If you cannot do it in practice, you will not be successful in competition. This is the single most important lesson you must learn.

In actual competition, you have to add the element of feeling, because without a high level of emotional energy, and deep commitment, you can't win.

A fencing bout is really a fight, only with some rules and protective gear so you don't get blinded or wounded. Let's assume you're serious and have worked hard to improve your technique, and have gained important bouting experience. You feel ready to take on better fencers, but progress is elusive, the problems above persist.

Here are the next set of problems, you are already fairly experienced, you know most of the moves your opponent makes, you're concentrating, you finally recognize a certain pattern, you even know which attack to make, but by the time you are ready to lunge, your opponent has moved to a new position. Your back foot was not in position to lunge. It needed another step forward before you could lunge with full power from the right distance. Or, you recognize another pattern, so you wait for it to appear again. But several opportunities pass that you were unable to take advantage of, because your mind was waiting for that first pattern to reappear. This is a common mistake we all make, but it is a very costly mistake that you must overcome. If your opponent is as good as, or better than you, you cannot afford to wait for the right opportunity to appear. You must create your own opportunities.

Have your mind free, which means being able to attack even when you are not sure what you will do, and make your repertoire broad enough, so you recognize a potential for attack, in almost every situation. This ability may take a long time to acquire because it is the mark of an accomplished fencer.

Most important, if you do not continually make serious threats to hit your opponent, you are allowing your opponent freedom to decide what he/she will do. If you give away the initiative, you will lose. If you cannot scare your opponent, you cannot beat him/her. When you scare your opponent, you will hit.

Or, your opponent attacks twice and scores both times. You don't know what to do, so you let the opponent attack again. Mistake! Now it's 3 to zero.

You must be able to retake the momentum in a bout, or simply lose. You must develop simple attacks the opponent cannot ignore, and be prepared to parry the riposté and at least not get hit. If your opponent makes a certain attack especially well, you cannot afford to let him/her use it. You must be able to prevent your opponent from doing what he/she wants to do, before he/she does it.

Once an opponent is able to do what they want, you have already lost; you have to fight off that feeling of depression, which will surely arise. This fencing situation is a battle for survival. Your opponent is going to kill you unless you kill him/her first. Thoughts like these have to arise from your feeling part; the mind only verbalizes the feeling, it is nothing but habitual talking in the head, and quite useless, you have already lost.

Keep your mind on making your opponent react to your aggression. Whatever move you try, make it for real. If you scare him/her they will try to parry. The opponent might parry so be ready, you must parry the counter action whatever it is, or the bout is lost. But make sure if the opponent doesn't parry, no matter what he does, you have to score the touché. Or the bout is lost. It may require two or three redoublements of your attack, so be ready to keep your concentration and your determination. It's 'do or die'. Your opponent may be better than you but he is going to know he has been in a fight. You have to keep being persistent until you start to win a few. You get better at it each time you try. Pretty soon you will be better than him/her. But don't forget, if this opponent is really any good, he/she will be getting better every time he/she fences you too. All good fencers, once beaten by someone, never forget, and will be out to kill you the next time you meet.

I was very lucky to fall into a situation where I met Michel Alaux. I was introduced to him by Abe Kadish, my high school fencing team Captain, and the man who taught me how to fence. Abe was on the varsity Epee team at NYU. He was also the one who told me to come to NYU for fencing. I was also lucky to meet Abe. One day he arrived in the practice room at NYU very excitedly, and told me, Herb, I just took a lesson last night from Michel Alaux at the NY Fencer's Club, he is fantastic, you have to meet him.

Michel Alaux was the Fencing Master at the Fencer's Club. A few years earlier he came here from France where he was the coach of Christian d'Oriola, the greatest foil fencer of the 20th century. Here in the US, Michel was destined to become US Olympic Fencing coach 5 times. I had the greatest coach you could possibly find. Abe was right, as usual, Michel was fantastic.

I learned the French Fencing system could be described in one word, 'position'. Later I met a foil fencer, Jon-Claude Magnan, who embodied the truth of that description. He too, won several World Championships, and Silver in the 1964 Olympics.

What does it mean, to describe a whole style of fencing with just one word? 'Position' means, that as much as possible, every part of the body should always be in the right place to make the touché. No matter what move you make, parry (all 8), lunge, advancing, retreating, ducking, turning, twisting, jabbing, the point of your weapon is pointed directly at valid target. No matter how wild the action may get you never miss hitting the target. This also means, you are always aware of where the point of your weapon is. Which also implies your body always moves as one whole unit, always pointing at the target. What it really means is your mind, body, and feelings, are always in 'position' to strike the target.

What is esoteric here, is that your mind, body and feeling are trained to function as a unified being, as much as possible. The unity of the three parts is what enables the fencer to move with blinding speed, total surprise and deadly accuracy. Because the point of your weapon is focused on some specific part of the valid target, the opponent's position is also included in your own self-awareness.

The fencer is always aware of a specific target that will be hit. This awareness, is not a plan of action in the mind of the fencer, but exists simultaneously in the present moment, as the fencer's own atmosphere. When a strike is made, the eyes, focused on the target, connect with the brain and then with the entire body, and movement is the result. There is no plan in your mind, and no plan for the opponent to figure out.

We all have a strong tendency to want to plan everything with our minds. This is the greatest obstacle we have to overcome. In fact, we never really overcome it. If you can manage to do it 10% of the time you will be amazed at the effect it has on your competitive results.

To let go of the head, trying to control everything, is extremely difficult to do. To a small extent, rigorous training in fencing lessons can raise the level of your technique to help you accomplish this. But when it comes to a struggle between really equal fencers, with equal levels of determination, well here, I can only say, 'may the best man/woman of the moment win.'

I will try a narrative from my personal experience, to express the experience of trying to let go of the head and allow the whole of myself take over, and make the touché. I was fencing Mike Gaylor in the finals of the 1968 Nationals. To my surprise I was losing 1 to 4, and was fighting my way back. I got to 4 - 4, I was worrying that I would lose. I remember being emotionally heightened, when I lunged into his low line. Mike leaped up and off to his right to avoid my point, and he was succeeding. But I saw my blade going right passed the target and redirected the point back onto the target to make the touché. As I recovered back to my en-gardé position I heard coming out of my mouth, 'how did I do that'!!! I rarely missed the target on a simple lunge, but Mike's jump completely surprised me, and in mid lunge, I could never redirect the point to hit. At least not ordinarily. As I redirected that point, I was in a higher state of alertness or being, than the person who later exclaimed 'how did I do that.' And yet to this day I can still visualize that point, as I saw the blade going passed the target and simultaneously redirected it to hit the target. But after that, as I was recovering from the lunge, I lost all memory of how it happened. I was back in my head, my ordinary state, commenting with a combination of words and emotion. And I remember that as well, as a memory.

A second example: I was fencing Albie Axelrod in the 1964 National finals. I had psyched myself up for this bout because he usually beat me. I had to beat Albie if I wanted a chance to win the Nationals. I resolved the only thing I wanted to accomplish in this bout, *was not to be afraid of him*, which I realized I usually was. The Director said 'ready, fence', Albie advanced and we crossed blades, my mind was blank, I was not afraid, I noticed he tapped my blade a second time, he hesitated, bam! I lunged full force at his chest and nailed him cold. I will never know exactly what happened or why, but I was able to make that touché only because my mind, and maybe my whole self was free in that moment. There was no plan, no thought. It was my greatest touché ever.

A third example, but not fencing: This event took place during the summer of 1959, in the Catskill resort area. I was working at the Funcrest Hotel. We travelled to a nearby hotel for a staff fencing match followed by a basketball game. A few of our staff were on their school basketball teams, and had training in how to play the game. Basketball was not a game I played recently. After we finished the fencing match, we began the basketball game. I was a substitute in the game, and was finally put in to play.

In spite of our team trying to pass back and forth to set up something in the right way, we were being slaughtered, because by the time we were ready to shoot the other team either stole the ball or blocked our shot. I came in grumbling 'we have to shoot not pass more'. I got my hands on the ball on the exchange and dribbled a few times moving toward mid court. I looked up and shot. My teammate alongside me yelled, 'what the hell are you doing'. I looked at him, and could still see the ball high in the air, 'we have to shoot' not pass. Swish! The ball went right in. He shut up.

On the next exchange I got the ball again to take it down court. Approaching mid court, I looked up again and shot. It went 'swish' again. Then it happened again, a third time. On the fourth time I noticed two pairs of legs in front of me, but I shot again and swish again. On the fifth time there were three pairs of legs in front of me. I remember thinking something, I don't remember exactly, but I was distracted, and I missed. I don't remember anything else about the game. I sank four straight shots. There's no way I could do that.

How do you explain that? Pure luck! Right, in terms of winning or losing the game, yes, pure luck. I don't recall anyone on either team mentioning anything about sinking those four shots. I may have been in a very special state, but no one seemed to notice, I guess only who won or lost, is all that mattered.

From an inner perspective I will never forget those moments, something in me was unified, at one with myself. Even if I had tried, which I never did, I could never repeat that feat. My ego would always be in the way, distracting me from being in a state capable of that feat. Even for a lot of money or no matter how hard

I would try I would not be able to do it again. So, who did it? And who is the one who could not repeat the feat? What do we call luck? What is luck?

I realize now, when I try to write about it, an explanation, based on a trinity concept, just might be appropriate.

I was upset the way my team was playing the game, even if we had little chance to win, if you don't at least try to shoot, what good is passing. So, I was emotionally angry at not having a chance to win. I was mentally unsatisfied by the team not using a decent strategy. And I was physically ready to shoot, since no one else was doing it. I was concentrated on the game, I wasn't thinking about what anybody else would think of me, for taking the shot. My teammate yelling out 'what the hell are you doing' was quieted when the first shot went in. I don't think I was egotistically involved, because basketball was not my sport. So, I leave it to you, to recognize the trinity elements, or not.

Writing has also stirred up many other childhood memories of sports events where the participation of mind, emotion and body, in a pure form seemed to lead to successful results.

To be or not to be.

These examples are what I mean by unexplained actions, or evidence for the reality of higher states of awareness or levels, or the results of the unity of the three centers, mind, body and feeling working together, or from the potential trinity within each of us.

Without doubt, one has to have one's own experience of moments like these, to even begin to question what is its significance. One particular question often arises when attempting an explanation: Who does this action? Is it you? Or, are you not the one who does it? Some other self within us? Someone does it.

Here's my answer: I want something very much, in this case maybe to win. I believe I see an opportunity, my whole body responds according to my training, the first moment I can, I shoot. It went in, I am stunned. I am following the action, I have the ball again, it worked, I am excited, I shoot again. It went in again. I am amazed, elated, just keep going. The same state is there, shoot again.   Finally, I am distracted, the mood is broken, I miss. Then I think in my head, wow, how did I do that? I am already in my usual thinking, walking, talking state.

Once experienced, I want to experience this again and again. But there is something about this that seems out of my control. I cannot repeat this state of heightened sensitivity, faster speed, and sharper awareness. All I can repeat are the words in my head, that I want to do it again. The words seem to take over, I keep repeating them, and actually these words are controlling me. I am repeating them obsessively. I am too tense, I have to calm down, remain alert, focus on the opponent, the situation. Patience, I cannot make it happen when I want, I have to allow for the opponent. I can pressure him/her but I have to be patient, let the right moment appear by itself. And be ready to pounce like a cat.

I have to recognize there are different states in which different results are possible. Hearing the words in my head is not the right state, or it means, I am in the wrong state. But even then, the right state is somewhere, but I don't know where, this is the mystery. And the mystery is what never goes away.

Chapter Eighteen,
The Esoteric Aspect of
Meditation

Meditation is exactly the opposite of trying to win something. But I suspect it is also exactly the same as trying to win something, only what I am trying to win is entirely within myself. I can say this, but I don't really know it.

Da Liu, my Tai chi Master, used to explain the difference between fighting and meditation as the same as the difference between Yin and Yang. With Yin one sits motionless outside, while the mind is active on the inside. With Yang one can be fighting on the outside, while one is calm and relaxed on the inside. Both states are extraordinarily difficult to attain. So, all we can do is try to discover the way or ways to approach the goal. The difficulty is, the more we try, the more we discover, the goal is my obstacle.

Only a small proportion of humans are interested in pursuing such paradoxical goals. I immediately think of these world-famous sayings, 'turn the other cheek', 'you have to die to be reborn', 'love your neighbor as yourself', 'to be or not to be', 'know thyself', 'there is a cloud of unknowing between you and God', 'be still, and know that I am God', "Life is real only then when 'I am' ", 'do unto others as you would have others do unto you'.

Somehow, it is hard to accept that the one thing I rely on, to encourage myself to succeed, is my Ego. I continue to expect that my next new technique, whatever it is, will unlock that magic door to what I seek. But each new approach turns out to be my old friend, Mr. Ego.

The real question is, will my Ego be strong enough to accept the humiliations I encounter, while being determined enough not to quit. I continue to think, if I could get rid of my Ego, everything else would be easy, 'a walk in the park'. But don't worry, we can't. Without our Ego we cannot even cross the street. So, forget a walk in the park. And remember, our Egos will be with us to the end. But also remember, if we do get the gist of meditation before we are ready to die, we just might have something that makes our journey worthwhile. The journey to fathom the hidden meanings in the world-famous sayings above, is at least a lifelong undertaking. So, like I said, the only thing I want to accomplish, is *not to be afraid*. (ref. Pg 92 fencing Axelrod)

Chapter Nineteen,
Meditation, Attention, Exercises

Don't take anything for granted, simple fear stops us from doing a lot more things than we are aware of. I am always a little afraid of failing. Even if it's as small as not keeping my own schedule. The other simple weakness I have, is laziness. This is so in spite of all the things I may have done, and even done well in my life. So, when I speak of exercises, don't laugh, very few people recognize their true value. Set up a schedule for doing a few minutes of exercises. Be sincere, can you approach a session without at least a moment of both fear and laziness? Is it a struggle, at least a little? If not, you are a stronger person than I am.

One word of special caution is about injuring yourself. To initiate an exercise routine is to make a big change for the body. Pushing too hard, especially in the beginning is a sure way to invite injury. Be very careful about knees and back, they are susceptible to twist and tear injuries.

How many days in a week? That's what you have to reach, do your exercise 7 days a week. That will take a while for you to accomplish. Maybe even a few years, like it took me, and then keep it up for years to come. If you can get this far, it won't matter what exercises you did, you will be strong and healthy. At least your body will have benefitted.

My exercises emphasize mind, working with body. So, if you follow a routine with my exercises, your mind will also be strong and healthy. The combination, mind and body, evokes feelings. One of the inner trinities is, 1 active: mind, 2 passive: strong, healthy body, 3 reconciling: joyful feelings.

But most important is that you should feel good, or great, after each workout. If you don't, don't quit too soon. As Americans, we are conditioned to try to do more than we should. We often over-do. Do exercises you like to do. It will take a while to find them, but it is worth the effort. It helps the body enjoy the workout. Over-doing sometimes brings minor satisfaction in the beginning, but if it isn't right for you, it will be replaced by strain and not wanting to do the exercise, whatever it is.

Each person is different and likes a different kind of exercise. It is well worth the effort to discover what you like best. If you listen to anything I say please make it this: most important is your resolve to keep fit throughout your life. 1. Mental resolve is active, 2. form of exercise is passive, 3. regular practice is reconciling. Regular means 7 days a week. Eventually.

Now I can tell you about the exercises that help sustain me. I do a combination of stretching; fighting postures, in slow motion; thigh strengthening; arm, leg, head, voice movements, controlled by the attention; turning, spinning or whirling exercise, also governed by the mind's attention. Each session takes from about 35 to 45 minutes. I try to do it every day. But when schedules change or the unexpected arises, I have to let it go. I have been doing it for the past 17 years.

Reference my 'YouTube' web site. Learn what to do by watching the exercises you are most interested in. What follows is a verbal description of the key points in each exercise.

STRETCHING: The basic idea is to prepare the body to move further than usual in all four directions. Done slowly, and enjoy. I do this first because it gives the least resistance.

With arms stretched out horizontally, turn from side to side, rotating with a back-and-forth movement.

With arms stretched upward and feet about 18" apart, stretch up and start bending backwards, stretching all the time. When you have stretched as far as you want to, lower your arms with the palms on the back of your buttocks. This supports your back as you stretch a little further.

Come out of the back stretch with arms vertical and begin a toe touch movement. Adjust feet to shoulder width and begin a forward stretch, slowly, down to touch the floor. Go down slowly and in gradual stages. Keep your knees as straight as you can, perfectly straight is not necessary. You want to eventually maintain the full downward stretch for as long as you can. This will significantly reduce stiffness in daily activity. Come up very slowly, feeling each vertebra, as you come to the upright position again.

TAI CHI: 48 postures, middle form, Yang style. This is only one of over 2,000 different styles and sequences. Consult Da Liu's book "Tai Chi Chuan and the I Ching". The 48 forms take me about 15-20 minutes to complete. Once you learn it, be mindful of where your attention is during the form. The focus should be at the point of striking in each form. Great for maintaining moderate leg strength and smooth relaxed flowing movements. Also helps open circulation to finer capillaries. Awareness of abdominal breathing brings increased mental calm and physical smoothness. The foot with the weight on it is 'Yin'. The foot with no weight or little weight on it is 'Yang'. Yin and Yang, heavy and light continue alternating throughout. One useful principle is always to make turns with weight on your heavy or Yin leg. Step and land lightly with your Yang foot. All moves are curved and circular. Also great for balance; and the smoothness helps you relax down to the very tips of your fingers. Doctors love Tai Chi because patients hardly ever injure themselves.

POWER THIGHS: After noticing how slow I was, at getting up from squatting, I was on the lookout for an exercise to strengthen my thighs. One day I saw Tyreek Hill, the fastest pass catching wide receiver in the NFL, doing his daily workout on TV. It attracted my attention because I was looking for an alternative to doing deep knee bends, which always ended up giving me painfully swollen knees. What Tyreek Hill was doing seemed like a perfect solution: He took a long step forward with the right leg and let his left knee touch the ground behind him. Then he pulled his left leg into another long step forward and let his right knee touch the ground behind him. This becomes a series of long steps forward with the back knee touching the ground behind him on each long step.

This is a great solution for strengthening your thighs without experiencing any knee discomforts. It is fully incorporated into my routine. But be careful about over doing it.

GURDJIEFF MOVEMENTS: without piano, with my modifications: The main purpose is to extend your ability to focus the attention. At the same time, different parts of the body make different movement patterns. These movements might be too difficult for many people. They can be very frustrating to try. You may give up, many, many times. But if you persist, your attention will become more able to include multiple different movements simultaneously. These exercises can also help to reduce mind wandering when trying sitting meditation. Much more I cannot say. I give no guarantees. You must do these exercises for the challenge alone.

When I was a child in Brighton Beach, Brooklyn, one of the children showed us a little game that must have been derived from some ancient tradition that knew something about the source of Gurdjieff's movements. It was called "pat your tummy, rub your head". Then you had to "pat your head, rub your tummy". Of course, back then I just dismissed it as a silly game. But I did try quite a bit to do it. Most of us were able to. And it does demonstrate that you have to pay attention to do it.

The simplest example is; with arms out, either to side, or front, swing the right arm up and down from shoulder height to waist, to a count of, 1, 2, 3, 4 etc.: with the left arm swing it the same way but with a count of, 1 2, 1 2, 1 2, etc. The left arm swings twice as fast as the right arm and makes 2 stops for every 1 stop of the right arm. Then reverse arms. Most of these exercises follow this principle. But I think it may be easier to watch the video to get the idea.

The most complex example is; doing each of the following simultaneously, step forward right left, step back right left, right turn 90 degrees, 4 times. Right arm takes 4 position patterns; Left arm takes 5 position patterns (See video) 4 times. Head takes a new position with each of the 4 turns; 1 down straight, 2 right straight, 3 left straight, 4 up straight. Mind speaks out once with each turn; Lord, have, mercy, on me. Whole exercise also done with different words on each turn: but words are done in cannon; I, can, wish, to be; can, wish, to be, I; wish, to be, I, can; to be, I, can, wish. Also, after each 4 turns, arms change from a 4 pattern to 5, and from 5 to 4. (See video)

Just as a reference, it took me 4 or 5 months to be able to do it. But it is still hardly ever perfect. It is a constant reminder of how weak my attention is. And, how difficult it is to sustain your attention.

INVENT YOUR OWN MOVEMENTS: If you are interested enough, invent your own movements. Once you get the idea of how these exercises stimulate and challenge your determination to develop the attention, you can start making up your own. Be creative, that's what this is all about. Discover yourself, and develop as an individual human being. Nothing is more exciting. And don't forget, the Biome is recording it all, so nature is preparing your future.

THE TURNING OR WHIRLING EXERCISE: As part of the Gurdjieff movement classes I took for over 50 years, we sometimes did the whirling Dervish exercises. They were usually done as the height and conclusion to a class. By then our attention was most alert. I always had the desire to do more of it. So, when Covid19 hit and I found myself stranded at home, I one day got the idea to begin including them in my routine. Apart from the many Gurdjieff classes where I participated in whirling, I never had any formal training in doing them.

However, I did see the Whirling Med Levi Dervishes from Turkey perform at The Cathedral of Saint John the Divine on Amsterdam Ave & W. 112 Street in NYC back in the mayor Lindsay days. And I did also get to see one or two other groups perform during the years. These were live performances and there was nothing to edit in or out.

The most stand out features of all these performances, to me, were first, how calm and relaxed each of the performers were, and secondly how each one had his (only men) own subtle, slightly individual style. They all also clearly enjoyed what they were doing. And although their joy was visible to the audience, they were not doing it for the audience. I believe it was the Med Levi Dervishes who announced at the beginning, that what we were about to see was in fact not a performance at all, but was part of the participants spiritual exercises. This was a Sufi group.

One thing I will warn you about is the fact that, yes, you can get dizzy and lose your balance and fall. So, you have to be careful where and how you whirl. I fell once badly. I was amazed how fast the patio ground came up to meet my, luckily outstretched hands, instead of my face. In losing the balance you have no stability; you are still spinning and have no control of where you are going. I really crashed. But I have not fallen even once since then. A few close calls, but I really learned to recognize the warning signs of being close to losing it. And I like my nose just the way it looks now.

In the Gurdjieff classes we always spun clockwise. However, all of the Dervish groups I have seen, both live and on video turned counter clock wise. At present I do not know why this is, or whether it matters at all. But I do know our Earth and all the planets in our Solar System turn counter clock wise. And Earth's rotation on its axis is also counter clock wise. So, in my own practice I do both, left and right turning. Both ways seem the same to me.

Interestingly, if you are turning right, and are getting ready to stop, if you turn left for several turns it completely eliminates the dizziness effect when you stop. In the beginning keep your eyes open. To try to turn with eyes closed, be careful, it is not that easy. But it is interesting to try with eyes closed. It highlights the question; do you know where your attention is.

While turning you can remain in one place or move in a circle. Moving in a circle is much more difficult. If you feel your mind is not focused enough you can try counting exercises while you whirl. An easy one is 1234,4321, 23455432, 34566543, up to 12 then down again 12 11 10 9, 8 9 10 11, 11 10 9 8, 7 8 9 10, 10 9 8 7, etc. A more difficult one is; count up and down at the same time... 1-100 2-99 3-98 4-97 etc. ... as far as you can. You can try different arm movements as you whirl. If you try head movements, be very careful, up and down, can easily make you lose your balance, suddenly and seriously. It is interesting to experiment, placing inner attention on your spine, or on your solar plexus. And be aware of your verticality.

I usually practice turning for from 4 -10 minutes. I did 20 minutes several times just to see if I could do it. It is not the most important thing. I cannot do any of these exercises perfectly. Each day my mood is different and the day is different and so is my exercise. I have never yet hurt myself doing any of these exercises, and I do not expect that you will either. This includes ankles, knees, spine, back, neck, shoulders, or arms. That's what is great about doing your exercises gently and carefully, you cause no harm.

If anything hurts while doing an exercise, slow down, or stop immediately. Pay attention to what hurts and try to figure out what is making it hurt. Do not ignore the area that hurts. Never try to forget the pain, it is trying to tell you something.

One last thought is my advice to begin each session with the easiest and most enjoyable exercise you plan to do. I find my resistance to doing the exercises is greatest before I start. So, I always start with the easiest so that the resistance is less, and quickly disappears.

Chapter Twenty,
My Experience the Moment
after Winning the 1964 National
Fencing Championship (Ch 4, Pg 40)

I remember the precise moment when I reached the goal of my first life's aim, to become a champion fencer. My approach was totally intentional. In 1963 I came in 5th, and I said to myself, next year, in 1964, I am going to win the U.S. championship. And I did it! You can imagine how great that would make me feel. Or anyone for that matter. There was only one problem, in the moment of winning, in a way that was beyond my comprehension at that time, I was shown, that I felt 'nothing' at all, and I was blank, nothing, empty. I also realized it was my Ego, alone, all by itself, that experienced the joy and elation of that moment.

Now, almost 60 years later, I wish to look back at that moment to see if I understand anything more about that life changing experience. Remember I am not trying to justify or rationalize anything, I just wish to comprehend the raw forces involved in my experience. My aim now is to see those forces, as they were in that moment, because in total that is who I was. Am I the same now, or could something be different. This very question came alive in me at that exact moment, and has been alive in me all these years since.

First a word about Ego, we all need an Ego, without one we cannot do anything or go anywhere. The job of the Ego is to place one's self first, and to have everyone else follow me, and agree with everything I think, and say, as the best, and right way to proceed. The problem is we live in a world where everyone else also has an Ego. So, if everyone's behavior was determined by their Ego alone, there would be even more heads bumping into other heads than there is now. Social life would become impossible.

Think about Ego as being a lot like Money, they are both necessary, but if that was all you needed to run things, there would only be chaos. The only form of government would be Dictatorship, and everybody would be miserable. There could be no freedom, or creativity, or cooperation, or progress. Ego, like money needs to be balanced and harmonized with mutual respect, recognition of talents and skills, integrity, honor of word and deed, good will and compassion for those who need help.

First, a word about racism, antisemitism, and all other narrowminded, unworthy, and prejudicious biases. The early 60's was a crucial time for the civil rights movement, and on the surface, I was aware of what was going on around me. Luckily for me I grew up pretty insulated from antisemitism. I had not met any Negro or Latino Americans yet. But my involvement in fencing changed all that very quickly. We had all kinds of boys involved in the New York City, P.S.A.L. sports program. There were no barriers on the fencing strip. One couldn't help learning, that how good you were at fencing had nothing to do with race or religion. This was obvious, pretty much to everyone. Each fencer I faced, presented a unique struggle with his particular size, strength, and capabilities. Smartness, cleverness, trickiness, intelligence and determination, all play a part in fencing, and actually in all sports. This personal experience made it clear to me that any claims to being superior, because of race or religion were sheer nonsense, and did not reflect reality or truth in any way.

However, what I was afraid of was bullying. It was my fear that if I beat people, they might beat me up outside, after the fencing was over. I really had to face this fear. My experience was quite surprising. What I actually encountered, was the fact that after defeating several opponents, they showed respect and admiration for my abilities. This gave me a lot of confidence, and renewed my faith in the good will, and decency of most people, at least with fencers.

Now, we can return to that strange experience of feeling 'nothing' when I became champion. I said earlier this event changed the course of my life. I began to read more widely and also began looking into various life improvement ideas and spiritual groups. Don't forget, this was the mid 1960's. Spirituality, with an Eastern influence, was flooding into the USA. And in NYC everything was available.

One of the methods I tried was the Gurdjieff work. It comprised weekly meetings with other people, spiritual movement exercise classes, and weekend work meetings outside the city, where we took on outdoor projects like gardening, painting, construction work, and crafts, like wood working, decorative iron shaping, and more. The main idea was to try to be more conscious of what we are doing, thinking and feeling. All this kind of work was entirely new to me, and I loved it.

One weekend our project was to dismantle a huge rented circus sized tent and return it. It was a big job and we had about 15 men working on it. We finally got the main part of the tent into a really big roll of canvas. A pickup truck was brought over to carry the huge roll away. But it became apparent it wasn't going to be too easy to get it up into the back of the pickup. About 6 or 8 of us were trying to figure out how to lift it into the truck. After a few minutes, and I remember thinking hard about how could we do this, I yelled out, let's get some wooden planks from the garage and lean them against the back of the truck so we can roll the canvass up onto the back. After a few moments, someone spoke up and said, 'sounds like a good idea, let's try it'. And we all went to do it. And it worked.

Totally, without expectation or intent, I began to have a warm, joyful experience rising up through my torso. And I felt myself saying to myself, 'this is what it feels like to be a man'. I was part of the team, I contributed, I was of value. It was this situation of being related with others, and really wishing to be part of it, that I needed. This is what was missing from my championship experience.

The experience of this energy rising up in me was unforgettable. Because of the spiritual circumstances of the work project, this experience was not trivialized, but stood as concrete evidence of a different possible state of experiencing life. At least for me! And it was the occurrence of this kind of experience that could be shared with others in our meetings. At times others would also share esoteric experiences so that a range of uncommon experiences could be exchanged together.

My experience encouraged me to continue along this spiritual path until today. I feel it has opened many doors to different aspects of life, and helped me comprehend much more about what I experienced when I reached my goal and became a champion in 1964.

What I have discovered is that there are at least two aspects of our individual lives that we need to be aware of at all times; one is our own natural gifts and abilities, and two is our personalities or Egos. How we manage these two aspects is more important than either one by themselves. I have written about harmony throughout this book, and a good definition of what harmony means, is precisely how well balanced an individual is with respect to these two aspects of life within oneself. The reconciling aspect, is how an individual interacts with one's neighbors, based on the first two aspects. If more people could live like this, our world would be much more harmonious.

Chapter Twenty-One, Doing what you Love, and Being more Conscious

Along with fencing at NYU in the afternoons, and at the Fencers Club in the evenings, I was able to maintain two evenings a week at the Gurdjieff foundation. I was active in several meetings each week. Being able to get rid of my computer job, and to coach fencing full time, was a long-time dream, and now I had reached it. Unfortunately, the opportunity came because my wonderful coach, Michel Alaux, was diagnosed with Cancer which led to his death about one year later.

At one of my Gurdjieff meetings, I brought up a question. I began to ask about the relation between doing what you love, and being more conscious.

The Gurdjieff teaching is all about how to become more conscious. And everybody knows, it is better to work at what you love, than to do something only for the money, or, to have to work at something you don't like. Now that I was working at what I loved, the question remained, was I becoming more conscious?

I brought up the question because when I actually stopped to look at it, I realized, that although I really did enjoy every minute of the fencing, now professionally, still, I had to admit, I didn't feel more conscious, or that I was becoming more conscious.

I recognized that my ego was quite delighted with my new position as Head Coach at NYU, and Fencing Maestro at the Fencers club. But being more conscious has to do with how you feel inside, and what you experience. On the outside my ego was clearly feeling happier. But seeing I didn't feel any more conscious inside, this question arose in me.

At that meeting, in response to the question I brought, my spiritual teacher or group leader responded, saying; you see, even with the right ingredients, in this case working at what you love, greater consciousness does not come about automatically. Only the ego benefits, automatically, from a favorable situation. Doing what you love frees something inside; you're not so filled with the strong negativity that can come from being forced to do something you don't like. So now you have to work inwardly, to search for that inner freedom, that could bring greater consciousness.

A Task of Remembering Yourself

She suggested I make it my task that week to try to 'remember myself' when I was working at fencing. This term, to 'remember myself' is one of the most important the Gurdjieff teaching uses, to refer to the intentional action of trying to be more conscious of everything inside as well as outside ourselves in a given moment. In a simple way, we mean the same thing when we say 'work' on yourself. In the Gurdjieff teaching, we make a clear distinction between the ordinary states of working, which are ruled by habits and conditioning, and the states of working consciously, where one's attention is more whole, and is more truly in the present moment, rather than wandering around in the past and the future. These different states can only be verified through one's own efforts and observations. These are the kinds of efforts and experiences we share in the group meetings.

So, I had my work cut out for me that following week. I was going to try to be conscious while I was teaching fencing. But first I had to choose a specific situation in which I would try to 'work'. I set for myself the aim of trying to 'work' when I began giving the one-on-one fencing lessons at the Fencers Club.

On the first day I was trying this, I went to NYU around noon, as usual, did my office tasks, got into my fencing outfit and began coaching various members of the team. On each of the three days I was to coach at the Fencers Club I would shower, change into my street clothes and take the subway uptown from NYU to the club, arriving a little before 5 pm.

At the club I would change back into fencing gear, and go out on the floor to start giving individual lessons. But on this night, while I was changing into my fencing gear, I reminded myself of the task. I had to 'remember myself'. Then I went out onto the floor. I began giving lessons. At the end of the evening, around 8 pm, as I was walking back to the locker room to shower, suddenly, I realized I had completely forgotten to do the task!

I was upset with myself, but I already knew it wasn't so easy to remember yourself, especially to do it precisely when you tell yourself you will. Yes, it may happen accidentally in life that you remember, but to do it with intention, one has to keep one's mind on the task. Well, I will try again.

The next night while changing at the club, again, I reminded myself. This time I said, ok, now stay with it, all right, I am remembering, and I was walking out onto the floor. I saw somebody, began talking, started my first lesson, but, the next time I remembered the task, I was back in the locker room, getting ready to shower and go home. I had completely forgotten again! I was mad again, but there was nothing to do but accept it, and resolve to try again.

On the third night, I was changing into my fencing gear, again getting ready to start my lessons. The task, and the fact I had forgotten the last two times, had been much on my mind. I was determined, not trying to force anything, but honestly, determined not to forget. I had to be very careful about getting distracted, and to remain alert. I got dressed, being very aware of what was going on around me, even aware of my own thoughts. I walked out onto the floor.

I said hello to my first pupil, I remained aware, we were both putting on our masks. I saluted her, she saluted me, I was still there very aware. I said to her, en-gardé, change beat in six, change, change, press back, feint disengage. I was still there, we began to move, and all of a sudden, I began to rise out of my body.

I was rising up above where I was giving the lesson, I was looking down and I was still giving the lesson. How could I be giving the lesson; I was up above looking down. I was in both places! I am looking down on myself giving the fencing lesson. I watched, I moved forward, the pupil retreated; then we began coming back. I watched my hand manipulate the foil; I was giving the pupil instructions; I was up at least 10 feet above where I was fencing below. I felt I was above, and I was also the body below, making fencing moves. This state lasted for a time, I don't know how long, maybe 30, 40 seconds, I am not sure.

I was so excited by this event I cannot tell you. The body is not all there is. I experienced it, I was in two places at once, and both were alive and active. Life is incredible, beyond what we know. At my next Gurdjieff meeting I shared it with my group. Our leader nodded her head, and continued; now you must go on, make use of this gift to intensify your efforts, to remember even more often.

For weeks, even months, I could not get this incredible event out of my mind. I was very happy, even ecstatic; I had been given confirmation that life on another plane exists, and is possible to experience. All this stuff about spirituality is true, in life, in the universe, spirituality is real.

Spirituality is true, but everyday reality is also true. The events of everyday existence and the continual struggle to survive is an ever-present reminder. It was clearer than ever that there is an inner world, and an outer world, and that we must include both. Michel had been happy for me, that having won the National Championship, I had something no one could ever take away from me. I felt the same way about this experience.

I have continued to 'work' for many years since then, but I have not yet had a repeat of this experience. In my opinion, it has something to do with being pure of mind and heart. My aim was to 'remember myself'; to keep my full attention on what was taking place within and around me. I had no thought about what might take place; I was working purely to be present. But now that purity is gone, and as my spiritual teacher told me, I have no choice but to move on, my ego knows about this experience too, and claims it as its own.

In an ironic way, my own ego continues to rob me of this experience. So now I have to find a way to 'work' that includes even my ego. And it comes to mind, that this is the dilemma all 'Adams and Eves' have to face when we get knowledge, and are no longer in the pure state of innocence, like in the Garden of Eden. Once we realize we are asleep, but can awaken, our responsibility becomes even greater.

With greater responsibility comes the luxury of choice. And true choice is a matter for our Souls, and our Consciences. And when we die, we will find ourselves in Fungi territory.

References

Suzanne Simard, The Hub Tree Documentary
A pioneer in Fungi research with many documentaries.
Check out YouTube

Paul Stamets, a self-educated and most famous of the pioneering Fungi researchers.
Producer of **'Fantastic Fungi'** and many other video documentaries.
Check out YouTube

Neil Diamond, His song, "Nothing but a Heartache"
From 2014 album "Melody Road"
Had a line that struck me as I heard it for the first time:
"But getting by don't mean you're living".
As I was writing, the line came into my mind.

Bibliography

The Lives of Fungi
A Natural History of our Planet's Decomposers
By **Britt A. Bunyard**
Princeton University Press 2022

All and Everything
Beelzebub's Tales to his Grandson
By **G. Gurdjieff**
E. P. Dutton & Co., Inc. 1964 Edition

The Bhagavad Gita
A Guide to Navigating the Battle of Life
By **Ravi Ravindra**
Shambala Publications, Inc. 2017

The Cloud of Unknowing
With the Book of Privy Council
The Author is: Anonymous, from Fourteenth
Century England
A new translation by **Carmen Acevedo Butcher**
(I think it is a great translation)
Shambala Publications, Inc. 2009

The Reality of Being
The Fourth Way of Gurdjieff
By **Jeanne de Salzmann**
Shambala Publications, Inc. 2010

Printed in the USA
CPSIA information can be obtained
at www.ICGtesting.com
LVHW040128270124
769484LV00016B/721